MW01028855

LIFE AFTER TERRORISM

"The guerrilla fights the war of the flea, and his military enemy suffers the dog's disadvantages: too much to defend; too small, ubiquitous, and agile an enemy to come to grips with."

—Robert Taber, *The War of the Flea* (1970)

"It is necessary to turn political crisis into armed crisis by performing violent actions that will force those in power to transform the military situation into a political situation. That will alienate the masses, who, from then on, will revolt against the army and the police and blame them for this state of things."

—Carlos Marighella, Brazilian guerrilla leader,
Minimanual of the Urban Guerrilla (1969)

"I swear by God the Great, America will never dream nor those who live in America will never taste security and safety unless we feel security and safety in our land and in Palestine."

—Osama bin Laden, October 7, 2001

"Currently, there is no credible information that a terrorist group has acquired, developed, or is planning to use chemical, biological, or radiological agents in the United States."

—Louis Freeh, Director of the FBI, May 10, 2001

Bruce D. Clayton, Ph.D.

Author of *Life After Doomsday*

N CIVILE

LIFE AFTER TERRORISM

What You Need to Know to Survive in Today's World

Paladin Press • Boulder, Colorado

Life Ater Terrorism: What You Need to Know to Survive in Today's World
by Bruce Clayton, Ph.D.

Copyright © 2002 by Bruce Clayton, Ph.D.

ISBN 1-58160-326-6
Printed in the United States of America

Published by Paladin Press, a division of
Paladin Enterprises, Inc.
Gunbarrel Tech Center
7077 Winchester Circle
Boulder, Colorado 80301 USA
+ 1.303.443.7250

Direct inquiries and/or orders to the above address.

PALADIN, PALADIN PRESS, and the "horse head" design
are trademarks belonging to Paladin Enterprises and
registered in United States Patent and Trademark Office.

All rights reserved. Except for use in a review, no
portion of this book may be reproduced in any form
without the express written permission of the publisher.

Neither the author nor the publisher assumes
any responsibility for the use or misuse of
information contained in this book.

Visit our Web site at www.paladin-press.com

TABLE OF CONTENTS

TABLE OF CONTENTS

WARNING

Although the information, opinions, and recommendations contained in this document are compiled from sources believed to be reliable, the author and publisher accept no responsibility for their accuracy, sufficiency, or reliability, or for any loss or injury resulting from the use of the information. Newly discovered hazards are frequent, and this information may not be completely up to date.

ACKNOWLEDGMENTS

"Thank you" to Gary Zimmerman for his trademark anal-retentive edit of the manuscript, and to Chuck Mosher for his technical review. I appreciate the help of the Wiseguys discussion group with my Internet research. Special thanks to my wife, Jeannie, for putting up with dinner-table conversations about anthrax, nuclear war, and other odd topics dear to my heart but not to hers. You make it all worthwhile.

PREFACE

Terrorists. Who are they? What do they want? Why are they shooting at us? Following the September 11, 2001, terrorist attacks on the United States these questions echoed across the nation. But one question was louder than the others: How can we protect ourselves?

Twenty-five years ago I started writing a book called *Life After Doomsday*, which explained how to survive a nuclear war.[1] It was my weekend hobby while I finished my doctorate in ecology. Years of research went into the book, and it was well received by its intended audience. In certain circles the book became known as "the bible of survivalism." It is still in print (and endorsed on hundreds of survival Web sites) two decades later.

My interest in emergency preparedness eventually led me into firefighting and then to the position of assistant director of the Office of Emergency Services for my rural county. In that position I attended numerous training classes about nuclear war, hazardous materials, and other threats to the community, including terrorism.

My duties as an emergency response planner required me to explore the world of terrorists and assess their potential for hurting my community. This research made me sensitive to subsequent news items as the terror situation developed over the next few years.

America has been under steady attack by terrorists for two decades, but for the most part we have ignored them. The same group that crashed the planes into the World Trade Center, the Pentagon, and the Pennsylvania countryside in 2001 declared a holy war on the United States in 1996 and has launched regular attacks on Americans ever since. In the meantime, we have had domestic terrorists attacking from the rear, in our very heartland. I have monitored these events with growing concern.

When I saw the Twin Towers collapse, I was dumbfounded and furious, just like you. The secret war was suddenly out in the open, and people needed to know how to deal with it. The news wires and talk shows buzzed with useless advice from the media's instant experts. Couldn't anybody do better than that?

To defend your family from terrorist attack, you need to draw on many different kinds of expertise. You need to understand the history of terrorists and their methods. You need to understand important aspects of chemistry, microbiology, genetics, physiology, and anatomy. You need expert advice about hazardous materials, radiological defense, and nuclear weapons effects. In terms of practical experience, it helps to have worn the self-contained breathing apparatus and knelt on the bloody pavement as a first responder. You need to know what emergency management and disaster response look like from the inside. You might find it comforting to know a thing or two about personal defense. To make your plans, you need the perspective that 25 years of survival preparations can give you.

I realized that most people do not have this breadth of expertise, but I do. I decided it was time for me to write another book. This book isn't for me. My survival preparations were made long ago. I hope you won't need the information contained in it either. However, when your children's lives are at stake, you can't afford to be ignorant, and you can't afford to make naïve mistakes. When your family is involved, survival stops being a game and takes on a grim seriousness. You need some advice from a friend who has been there.

Knowledge is power. Knowledge and experience trump gadgets and theory every time. *Life After Terrorism* will teach you, amuse you, and make you think. It will, also, probably make you mad. I hope you won't be quite the same person when you finish reading it.

—Bruce Clayton
July 1, 2002

PART I

Terror in America

The goal of *Life After Terrorism* is to examine strategies that make our families less vulnerable to the threat of terrorist attack on U.S. civilians. Every threat analysis begins by defining the problem. If the problem is misunderstood, the solutions are worthless.

Part I is a survey of terrorists, their weapons, and their targets. Who are they? How do they attack? What targets do they prefer?

CHAPTER 1

AMERICA AT WAR

When did you first realize that terrorists were stalking America? Do you remember the moment?

For most of us it was September 11, 2001. We will never forget seeing that second airliner punch a hole in the south tower of the World Trade Center. *That's no accident,* I thought, watching the news that morning. *We're being attacked!* Were you taken by surprise like so many others? Did you think, *That's an act of war?*

Maybe the 9/11 attacks didn't catch you by surprise. Maybe you were tipped off by the suicide bombing of the USS *Cole* in Yemen, on October 12, 2000, when an Islamic fanatic almost sank a U.S. warship. Blowing up a warship is an act of war, too, isn't it? Were we fighting a war?

Or you might have awakened to the threat the previous December (just before the millennium) when an Algerian,

Municipal employees in an antianthrax training exercise in Antibes, France, on Friday, October 19, 2001. Putting on the suit is easy. Taking it off later is the dangerous part. (AP Photo/Lionel Cironneau.)

Ahmed Ressam, was arrested at the U.S.–Canadian border with more than 100 pounds of explosives in his car. Ressam admitted he was planning to set off a large bomb at Los Angeles International Airport on New Year's Day.

Maybe you noticed the arrest of Arab terrorists in Jordan about the same time? They were planning a millennium attack on a hotel full of American tourists. There was also a plot to set off a bomb in the crowd in Times Square that same New Year's Eve. Surely, you knew then that we were fighting a war.

I know that you remember the twin bombings of the U.S. embassies in Nairobi, Kenya, and Dar es Salaam, Tanzania, on August 7, 1998, which killed 258 people and injured more than 5,000.[1] The United States launched cruise missiles in retaliation, striking terror training bases in Afghanistan and destroying a chemical factory in Sudan that reportedly produced nerve gas for terrorists. The fact that we fired missiles into *two sovereign nations* surely alerted you that we were at war? Knowing that the Islamic terrorists could make *nerve gas* tipped you off that the Americans were in serious danger, right?

Maybe you had noticed the terror war two years previously on June 25, 1996, when a car bomb exploded just outside the Khobar Towers apartment complex in Saudi Arabia, a U.S. military residence, killing 19 servicemen and injuring 400 others. Or maybe you noticed the car bomb that killed five American servicemen in Saudi Arabia the year before that, on November 13, 1995. *People are killing our soldiers,* you may have thought. *We must be in a war!*

Of course, we were all placed on alert the *first* time Islamic radicals tried to collapse the World Trade Center, on February 26, 1993. Six Middle Eastern men were apprehended, tried, and convicted of killing six persons and wounding 1,040 others with a car bomb in the World Trade Center basement parking area. Investigation of the bombing revealed that it was part of a larger plan that included *hijacking an airliner and crashing it into CIA headquarters.*[2] We heard that plan described in court in 1994 at the trial of the terrorists.

Were we paying attention? Could the warnings have been any more clear? These attacks were all mounted by Islamic fundamentalists, mainly at the instigation of Osama bin Laden and his shadowy al Qaeda network. Al Qaeda declared war on U.S. servicemen in 1996 and on all U.S. civilians in 1998.[3] We know because they said so, loudly and publicly.

And on Tuesday, September 11, 2001, they took us by *surprise?*

If so, it may have been because we hear about too many terrorist incidents. They are always in the news. In fact, the U.S. Department of State estimates that more than 9,000 terrorist incidents have occurred in the world since 1980. That figure *excludes* incidents involving Palestinians.[4] It also ignores U.S. domestic terrorism.

Where will they strike next? How can we protect ourselves? What will we do when—not if—they attack our nation again? Suddenly these questions are on everyone's mind.

To meet this challenge, we have to know our enemy. What do they want to do? What can they do? What will they do? Finally, what can we do to prepare? To find the answers, we have to study the fanatics, their tools, and their goals.

We can be certain that *they* are studying *us.*

CHAPTER 2

THEORY OF TERRORISM

Americans are baffled by terrorism. We can't imagine why anyone would kill civilians. We consider it a personal tragedy when a major military bombing operation accidentally kills one innocent bystander. America has impressive strengths, but we face the world armed with the sword of innocence and the shield of ignorance. At least our hearts are pure.[1]

What is terrorism? Who are these guys? *Why* do they hate us?

WHAT IS TERRORISM?

In recent years, our politicians and reporters have trivialized the word *terrorism* by applying it to every act of violence, intimidation, and confrontation. We have come to the point where anyone who owns a gun is a terrorist. Abusive husbands are terrorists. Playground bullies are terrorists. We have become the victims of our own hyperbole. We also refer to organized crime syndicates as terrorists. Street gangs are terrorists. Kidnappers and extortionists are terrorists. This reflects a deep misunderstanding. Terrorism is not about violence, and it is not about money. It isn't even about hate. Terrorism is about power.

Terrorism is a political tool used by ruthless and ambitious men to build personal power.

When you understand the terrorist's goal, you can predict what he is going to do. Generally speaking, terrorists do not arrange atrocities because they hate their victims. Usually the terrorist leaders don't really care about the victims. They care about embarrassing a government, eroding that government's power and legitimacy, and swelling the ranks of their own organization. The more soldiers you have, the more power you have. Ultimately, most terrorists hope to become the government. Now and then they succeed.

TOOLS OF TERRORISM

The twin tools of terrorism are a *noble cause* and a *deep hatred*. Terrorist leaders manipulate these tools with great skill.

In this definition of terrorism, the true terrorists are the leaders. They use the tools of terrorism to attract and manipulate rank-and-file soldiers. If you want ignorant young men to follow your banner, you must give them a noble cause to fight for and an enemy to hate. The cause legitimizes the hatred, and the hatred makes the soldiers willing to kill and die at your command.

Sometimes the selection of the enemy is dictated by circumstances. Revolutionaries hate the ruling government. Resistance fighters hate the occupying army. Sometimes the hated enemy is society at large or free enterprise or communism or Jews or the Romanovs or African Americans or Protestants or policemen or abortionists or people who eat meat. The enemy can be practically anything that can serve as a convenient focus of hatred.[2] The terrorist leader cynically fuels this hatred. It is easier if there are real grievances to exploit, but it is not necessary. Ignorant and envious young men will believe practically *anything* if it is sufficiently outrageous. When the terror organization grows large enough to take over local education, the hate training begins in earnest. In 10 years you have a population of teenagers who have never known a balanced view of history. In terms of the Taliban, their pupils spend eight years reading *one book*.[3]

The noble cause? Rescue our nation! Defend our faith! Avenge our dead! Liberate our brothers! Freedom! Equality! Brotherhood! Death to tyrants! These are all noble causes that amplify hatred. My favorite is, "Free the Holy Land from the infidels!" Those are the words that launched the Christian Crusades. A thousand years later, Islamic militants used the identical words to launch their terror war on the United States.

WHY TERRORISM WORKS

The strategy of terrorism works because it creates a positive feedback loop that makes the terror organization more and more powerful with each cycle. Throughout the middle of the 20th century, communist insurgents toppled one government after another using these tactics. The situation is more complex when the terrorists strike from outside a country, but the basic elements are the same.

11

Terror from Within

To overthrow a government, domestic terrorists begin by attacking defenseless, innocent people. Often it is just a bomb in a public place. Sometimes it is a hijacking. Sometimes they stop a random bus and shoot all the blue-eyed passengers. It doesn't matter. The deaths are outrageous, and an angry public *demands* better protection from its government.

The only way the government can respond to this demand is by imposing inconvenient and often humiliating security precautions on the public. This gradually builds a wave of resentment against the government. The resentment convinces a few wavering malcontents to join the terrorists. Those who remain on the fence ease their consciences by making monetary donations to charities that secretly (or openly) support the terrorists. The terrorist has more men and material to work with and starts to plan the next attack.

People are willing to put up with document checks, searches, and other indignities as the cost of improved security, but what if the terror continues in spite of the new precautions? Another post office is blown up. Another airliner is hijacked. Another busload of tourists is massacred. How does the public react?

The public reaction, perversely, is to lash out at the government for failing to protect them. Responding to this criticism, the government tries even harder to improve security and eventually begins to treat every citizen as a potential terrorist. The government establishes a secret police force to capture and torture suspected terrorists. Most of the people they torture are innocent. This results in even more public resentment against this oppressive, heavy-handed, and *ineffective* government. That gives the terrorists even more resources to work with so that they can stage a larger atrocity next time. That produces an even more brutal crackdown, which generates even *more* support for the terrorists. With

AIRPORT SECURITY

In the aftermath of the 9/11 disaster, Americans angrily demanded better airport security. The federal government swung ponderously into action.

Airport security guards have orders to confiscate "weapons" from passengers, including plastic knives, nail files, and fingernail clippers. Their unstated assumption is that you need a weapon to hijack an airliner. Has it occurred to you that a terror group that can field 19 suicidal hijackers at the same time *doesn't need weapons* to hijack a plane? They can buy tickets for any number of soldiers, march them through the strictest airport security, and take over the airliner with their bare hands.

The Federal Aviation Administration plans to counter this threat by putting one lonely sky marshal on each flight. (Six bullets divided by 19 hijackers is . . . not enough.) Note that airport security equipment cannot detect a bulletproof vest.

The same security personnel also search the *pilots* of the aircraft. One pilot had a pair of souvenir chopsticks confiscated from his flight bag. Congress says pilots can fly the aircraft and can carry guns in the cockpit, but we're going to search their luggage anyway. They might be carrying forbidden chopsticks.

Finally, did you know that 87 percent of the security guards at Washington, D.C.'s Dulles Airport are *not* U.S. citizens? The Equal Employment Opportunity Commission recently ruled that the airport security firm *must* employ Arab noncitizens as security inspectors and be sensitive to their religious needs.[4] Six of the Arabs in question were citizens of Sudan and one of Afghanistan.

Does all this activity make you feel safer, or does it make the government seem confused and stupid? The whole point of a terrorist attack is to undermine our faith in the government. It works. Attempts to increase internal security always make the government look bad.

every cycle, the government loses legitimacy, and anyone opposed to the government gains credibility.

At some point the terrorists assume the role of heroic freedom fighters, defending the helpless masses from the fascist government. Volunteers eagerly flock to the noble cause. At this point, people are so upset with the government that nobody remembers who struck first. If you remind them, they don't believe you.

Late in the process, the frustrated government officials commit atrocities of their own. At that point they have lost the game. After they have bombed a few civilians, abandoned due process, and burned down a few houses, they can never reclaim the moral high ground. Government credibility and power go into a downward spiral. The next step is open revolution.

Does this theory actually work in real life? There are plenty of historical examples. I have included a sidebar on airport security (page 13) to see whether the September 11, 2001, attack has begun to erode your faith in the government. The language is deliberately provocative, as terrorist recruiting messages tend to be.

Faced with terrorists, governments generally make themselves look evil and stupid. Our government is no exception. The terrorists will attack again. Federal precautions against terror will escalate while seeming ever more ineffective. As a tool for discrediting a government, the terror process works.[5]

Terror from Without

If the terrorists attack from *outside* the target nation, as is the case with Islamic militants attacking the United States, the same basic pattern emerges.

The strategy of international terror is rather clever, because it lets the terror organization grow in relative safety under the protection of a local government. This is short-sighted on the part of the hosting nation because a successful terror organization eventually becomes an army and terror armies have to be used against *nearby* targets. If militant Islamic fundamentalists are growing an army in the Middle East, it is because they have military ambitions *in the Middle East.* The attacks on the United States are actually part of a campaign to overthrow moderate Islamic governments (and non-Islamic governments) stretching in a broad band that includes Nigeria, northern Africa, the Middle East, the Indian Subcontinent, Indonesia, and the Philippines. The noble goal is a coalition of extreme Islamic governments, the new caliphate, which will expel the "infidels" from Saudi Arabia and Israel.

The Middle Eastern terrorists have no plan to overthrow the U.S. government. Even so, their attacks on U.S. targets serve to discredit the government and create a fertile environment for domestic "resistance" groups to gain support and credibility. The side effects of the attacks are as dangerous as the attacks themselves because they provoke government security efforts and inflame resistance movements at the same time.

DANGER OF OVEREXTENSION

A terrorist leader faces one serious danger: becoming too big. He is a success in fighting "the war of the flea" because the flea is agile and small and takes small, annoying bites. He isn't easy to find, and he isn't worth chasing. Both of these factors are eroded as the terror organization becomes larger and starts to do more serious damage.

Terror campaigns court disaster when the soldiers of the night become too numerous and coalesce into an army. You can't hide an army. You have to build bases for an army. You have to feed an army. You have to equip an army. Worst of all, an army with a noble cause and a hated enemy will *turn on you* if you don't let it fight somebody.

15

As the terrorist leader, you could lose your power—not to mention your head.

The terrorist leader often solves this problem by letting his soldiers attack someone not too dangerous. This could be a rival faction, an ethnic or religious minority, or the government that hosts you in your exile. This is one reason that terrorists don't make good guests. The leader keeps this brush war simmering with raids and skirmishes, but not battles. You can lose a battle. There is *no military purpose* to the raids. The leader uses the raids to keep his own people motivated but under control.

For one thing, the terror leader uses brush-war raids to liquidate anyone who emerges as a rival. The potential rival gets the "glory" of leading the raids. He soon becomes a martyr to the cause, instead of a living threat to the current leadership. As the commander of the September 11 hijack teams, Muhammad Atta would have been the greatest hero in the Middle East if he had lived. Instead, he died at the controls of the first plane to hit the World Trade Center.

In this context, the United States has always been a pretty safe enemy for terrorists to attack. The terrorist can dispatch his minions to blow up a U.S. embassy or aircraft in any remote corner of the world. These attacks satisfy the bloodlust of the soldiers, provide good public relations for the movement, and are perfectly safe. What's the United States going to do? Send ships halfway around the world and *invade?* Don't be silly.

For this reason, it is a mistake for a terrorist group to do too much damage. Small attacks serve the purpose. Large, damaging attacks make it worthwhile for the target government to move ships, launch planes, write new laws, suspend civil liberties, and send in soldiers. A big success can be fatal to the terrorist.

Success is dangerous in other ways, too. When a terrorist revolutionary actually wins the war, he deposes a government. This is a disaster for two reasons. First, an oppressive enemy is the *sine qua non* of the terror mechanism. Without the hated enemy, the terror organization dissolves and goes home. The power melts away. It becomes imperative to find a new enemy! Note that the United States was the best friend of the Afghan resistance until the Soviets pulled out and went home. Within a couple of years, the United States became the Great Satan, the new enemy.

When you replace a government, you have new responsibilities to your people. At first the people love and trust you because you are the champion of the little man. You defeated the hated enemy. You achieved the noble goal. You are the savior! Unfortunately, to run a country you have to set policies and make compromises, which are skills foreign to autocratic terror leaders. These policies will be too strict for some and too lax for others, and suddenly your own terror organization splinters and the extremists denounce you. One day, a bomb blows up a bus full of children, and your outraged citizens demand protection! When you cannot protect them, they lose their faith. The power of your government starts to erode, and the terror cycle continues.

TYPES OF TERRORISTS

Who are these guys anyway? Without descending to the level of individual personalities, we can classify terrorists into half a dozen major types.[6] This provides a basis for examining their access to weapons and choice of targets.

Lunatic Loners

Most Americans asked to name a domestic terrorist would instantly finger Timothy McVeigh, who blew up the Alfred P. Murrah Federal Building in Oklahoma City on April 19, 1995, killing 168 people and wounding hundreds more. After a moment's thought, they would add Ted

Kaczynski, the Unabomber. If you suggest Larry Wayne Harris as a third example, they say, "Who's he?" Harris is an eccentric biologist who bought a bubonic plague culture by mail order and then boasted to his friends that he was creating a bioweapon.

In my opinion, these three men were *not* terrorists, but their adventures tell us a lot about terrorist capabilities:

- If an angry loner like Timothy McVeigh can blow up a federal building with a car bomb, then an organized terror group can do it, too.
- If a paranoid schizophrenic like Ted Kaczynski[7] can evade the FBI for 16 years while sending homemade bombs to professors and business executives, then other terrorists can make bombs and evade capture, too.
- If an eccentric microbiologist like Larry Wayne Harris can purchase a bubonic plague culture by mail, or recover anthrax spores from contaminated soil, then terror groups can obtain dangerous disease cultures, too.[8]

If one guy can do it alone, then certainly an organized, well-financed team can do it. (In fairness, Harris isn't in the same league as the other two. McVeigh got death. Kaczynski got life. Harris got five weeks of community service.)

In my opinion, McVeigh and Kaczynski were lunatics, not terrorists. They were loners, not leaders. Although they could frighten and kill, they could not build an organization that could topple a government. In McVeigh's case, though, other organizations profited by his acts: the publicity surrounding his trial and execution seems to have provided new recruits to the domestic militia movement.

Fringe Groups
The United States is a hotbed of fringe political groups. They are always there, usually fueled by some noble cause

and a large dose of hate for somebody, but most of the time they are not well organized. With the right leadership, one of these groups could become a terror cell, so the FBI keeps a pretty sharp eye on them. Considering the number of extremists out there, it is surprising that we don't have more trouble from them.

As an informed citizen, you should be aware that large political movements naturally spawn extreme splinter groups. Political action groups (such as ecology, pro-life or animal rights groups) serve a legitimate purpose in airing their issues. Simply by existing, however, these movements create a forum where extreme individuals can meet one another and band together. These extremists are the vocal militants who are never happy with partial solutions and compromises. Eventually they break off to form splinter organizations that are more extreme than the parent. When a splinter group grows large enough, it spawns an even more extreme group.

This process gradually distills the most extreme fanatics into a genuine terrorist cell. The process is as natural as rain and can occur with any political ideology that has a noble goal and a hated enemy. The fringe groups don't expect to overthrow the government—instead they hope to overthrow human nature. It is useful to think of them as organized lunatics who can do damage but cannot effect change.

Louis Freeh, who served as director of the FBI from 1993 to 2001, recently said, "Special interest extremists—most notably within the animal rights and environmental movements—have turned increasingly toward vandalism and terrorist activity in attempts to further their causes." For instance, the Earth Liberation Front (ELF) claimed responsibility for eight acts of arson at Vail, Colorado, in October 1998 that caused $12 million in damages. ELF claimed that the fires were in retaliation for the resort's planned expansion that, it said, would destroy the last remaining habitat in

Colorado for the lynx. (Does this sound like an effective strategy to you?)

The pro-life antiabortion terrorists belong in this category, too. It's the same picture: the noble cause and the focal hate. This has led to abortion clinic bombings and the murder of a doctor by a sniper. The scale of the antiabortion violence is very small, with only a few individuals involved in serious attacks, but it involved threats of anthrax letters years before the first genuine anthrax letters appeared. The pro-life movement is not a "fringe" group, but it provides an environment in which fringe personalities can meet and encourage one another to do extreme acts.

One more example sounds like something out of a Tom Clancy novel.[9] As far back as 1972, the FBI infiltrated and broke up an ecoterrorist group called R.I.S.E. (the meaning of the acronym was never determined). R.I.S.E. planned to use typhoid fever, diphtheria, dysentery, and meningitis to exterminate all of mankind.[10] Its plan was to kill off most of humanity to prevent the destruction of nature and then start over again with a select few. The leaders of the group escaped to Cuba, where one died. The other eventually returned to the United States and went to prison.

Religious Cults

This nation is dedicated to religious freedom, which makes our society one of the strongest and most enlightened in history. It is a little hard to say, though, where religious freedom ends and cultism begins. The definition of a cult is a group of people living communally, which is ruled by a single charismatic leader who propounds an extreme religious viewpoint. David Koresh and the Branch Davidian Church of Waco, Texas, come to mind. (I narrow the focus here for the purposes of this discussion.) In terms of terrorism, a cult is a religious group that teaches hate instead of love.

Now, was David Koresh a terrorist? He had an end-of-the-world vision, but did he attack anyone? In my opinion, people who build their own prison compounds and move into them have done society a service. The appropriate response should be to put up "quarantine" signs around the neighborhood to keep neighbors and deliverymen at a safe distance. The guys in the bunker should like that; if they want to withdraw from the world, let them. It's irresponsible to fulfill their fantasies by digging them out at gunpoint. And for what? To move them from one prison to another?

Now and then a cult leader decides that society needs to be punished. Becoming intoxicated with power, he convinces his group that murder is a religious virtue. Just look at the Tate–LaBianca murderers who did it all for Jesus, in the person of Charles Manson. That true believers can be the most dangerous people on earth is shown by the actions of the Aum Shinrikyo cult, a Japanese group that made history in 1995 by releasing sarin nerve gas on five Tokyo subway trains during the morning rush hour. The cult killed a dozen people and injured about a thousand. Why? The members had a twisted religious agenda—and a charismatic leader.

Aum Shinrikyo was founded by a blind acupuncturist, Shoko Asahara.[10] One day, Asahara was struck by the realization that he was the reincarnation of the Hindu god Shiva, "the destroyer of worlds." Asahara established a large cult (10,000 followers in Japan alone) and founded a cult-staffed software company that generated millions of dollars. He believed that average Japanese citizens should be sacrificed to bring about the end of the world; killing an unbeliever was beneficial to the souls of killer and victim alike, he said. Using money donated by members and from the proceeds of the software company, Aum Shinrikyo set up a laboratory for making its own chemical and biological weapons.

Between 1990 and 1995, Aum Shinrikyo launched 10 chemical attacks on the public (using sarin, VX, phosgene, and hydrogen cyanide) and seven biological attacks (with anthrax and botulinum toxin). The cult also used VX to murder 20 dissident cult members, and there were many additional incidents where Aum's role was suspected but not proved. (The cult also made an art of injecting opposing lawyers with syringes of nerve poison.)

There are three lessons to be drawn from the Aum Shinrikyo phenomenon. The first is that the right religious leader can convince followers to do anything, even murdering innocent people in cold blood (also Asahara permitted the inner core of Aum Shinrikyo to drink nothing but his own bathwater and semen.) Second, a large enough terrorist group can generate a lot of money, more than enough to build or purchase serious weaponry. Third, with all this going for them, Asahara's zealots were remarkably ineffective killers. Why was that?

The Aum terrorists committed many individual murders, but their attempts at causing mass casualties were pathetic. For instance, their anthrax and botulism bacteria turned out to be special strains that were harmless. Their sarin was deployed as a liquid in plastic bags, not as an aerosol or spray. The people who died in the famous subway attack were the train officials who picked up the wet baggies to throw them away. The cyanide bombs Aum members left in subway restrooms never went off. In many of their chemical attacks nobody was injured. People reported a "bad smell," and that was all. Why so little success?

We know for a fact that one Aum Shinrikyo attack failed because an insider sabotaged it—the botulinum toxin was secretly replaced with water before the attack. Sabotage might account for some of the other failures, too, such as bombs that never went off and bacterial cultures that couldn't infect anyone. Aum Shinrikyo is often held up as evidence that it is impossible for amateurs to make their own chemical and biological weapons, but their failures might have been due to sabotage by their internal dissidents, of whom 20 were murdered. A more cohesive group might have had greater success. About 100 of the Aum Shinrikyo inner core were eventually arrested. Some have been hanged, and the trials will go on for years. The cult continues under another name and new leadership but with the same apocalyptic vision. Authorities keep a nervous eye on it. Even with Asahara imprisoned for life, membership is growing.

Revolution and Resistance

The classic terror mechanism is as old as time. You can see it in the Robin Hood legend. Robin and his Merry Men conducted lightning raids against the oppressive Normans, who obliged them by cracking down on the Saxon peasants. The legend paints Robin as the champion of the oppressed Saxons but doesn't point out that his raids directly brought about their misery. Robin Hood is a myth, but he was drawn from life.

Resistance fighters often adopt terror tactics to tire out occupying armies and convince them to go home. The mujahideen used terror against the Soviet occupation in Afghanistan during the 1980s. Hit, run, disappear. Let the soldiers take out their frustration on the civilians, who then join the resistance. Osama bin Laden was prominent in that fight, and it should be no surprise that some people of Afghanistan regarded him as a folk hero and protector of the masses, much like a Robin Hood.

Ireland is practically the archetype of resistance through terror. The ongoing terrorist campaign in Northern Ireland dates back at least to 1610, when England deliberately "colonized" Ulster by offering free land to thousands of puritanical Scots. The displaced Catholic Irish saw this as an invasion. Irish nationalists under various banners have spent *four centuries* trying to repel the invaders through alternating cycles of wars, rebellions, intrigues, and terrorism.[12] The net result is that most of Ireland is now independent of British rule, leaving the Orangemen (descendants of the Protestant colonists) under siege in their northern redoubt. The Irish, the Orangemen, and the British are gradually finding compromises and political solutions, but members of the hardcore Irish resistance remain dedicated to their noble goal and their implacable hatred, even though every hand is against them at the moment.

We have exactly the same situation in Israel, except that the "invasion" occurred gradually between 1897 and 1947. Jewish Israeli settlers displaced Islamic Palestinians. When the United Nations recognized Israel as a new nation in 1948, neighboring Islamic nations launched wars to drive out the invaders, and they lost. Resistance movements formed and have waged unending terrorism since then. You can see the terror mechanism at work in the militarily pointless raids, ruthless crackdowns, and deliberate education of Palestinian children to hate Israel and admire terrorist martyrs. When will we finally have peace in Israel/Palestine? The Irish have been fighting the Orangemen for 400 years. In comparison, the Palestinians are just getting started.

We should also take a look at the new wave of homegrown resistance organizations, often called "militias." The United States has always had a few diehard right-wing militants who persisted through every administration and social condition, usually guided by a noble goal (such as patriotic, racial, or religious purity) and an irrational hate (usually for Blacks or Jews and their "minions" in the U.S. government).[13] They had many recruits among impoverished farmers in the 1970s and actively recruited tax protesters in the 1980s. Since the Ruby Ridge shootings and the Branch Davidian disaster at Waco, however, they have become self-styled champions of liberty in the face of oppression. Their ranks have grown enormously.[14]

The militia rank and file see themselves as noble resistance fighters protecting America from a dangerous government. This is the natural backlash to the actions of the FBI and BATF, and provides yet another example of terrorism at work. A few extremists provokes a heavy-handed response from the government, and the bloodshed generates armed support for the extremists. This appears to have taken the government completely by surprise, as it usually does.

It is very important for the future of our country that we not allow that cycle to be repeated. There are, after all, other compounds like the Branch Davidian ranch in Waco. A true terrorist leader will try to force the FBI into another confrontation, but federal authorities would be very wise to decline that invitation. The peaceful resolution of the 81-day standoff with the Montana Freemen in 1996 was a good sign.[15]

In the context of the militia movement, let me offer you a bit of historical perspective. *Real* resistance fighters don't build forts, put on snappy uniforms, and pose in front of cameras as some of the militia leaders do. Resistance fighters blend in and make themselves invisible.[16] Let's keep that in mind as events unfold.

State-Sponsored Terrorism

During the Cold War, we witnessed the spectacle of two superpowers sponsoring insurgent movements all over the world. I refer to the Soviet Union and Red China, both of whom were ideologically committed to spreading communism throughout the Third World. To this end they fostered and supported revolutionary movements in many countries, and these incipient revolutions used terror tactics to build support. In Nicaragua, the Sandinista campaign to topple the Somoza government with Soviet support fit this pattern. So did the subsequent U.S.-supported Contra campaign to topple the Sandinistas.

And then the Cold War ended, the Soviet Union collapsed, and the Chinese developed internal problems. There was a remarkable drop in international terrorism. You hardly ever hear about guerrilla wars in the news any more. State-sponsored terrorism still persists, however, as a means for certain nations to promote their strategic interest in situations where they don't want to risk too much and would prefer to deny responsibility.

Every year the U.S. Department of State issues a report on trends in terrorism. In the 2000 edition, six countries were names as sponsor states that keep the terror teapot simmering.[17]

- Iran is the leading sponsor of terrorism, according to the U.S. State Department. It provides support (with varying amounts of funding, training, and weapons, as well as some sanctuary) to numerous terrorist groups that seek to undermine the Israel–Palestine peace negotiations. Iran also provides a lower level of support (funding, training, and logistics assistance) to extremist groups in the Persian Gulf, Africa, Turkey, and Central Asia. Although the $2.8 million contract put on the head of author Salman Rushdie by the late Ayatollah Khomeini is still technically open (the current popularly elected Iranian government has no authority, it says, to reverse a religious *fatwa*), in 1998 the government announced that it no longer encouraged the assassination of Rushdie.
- Iraq provides safe haven and support to a variety of Palestinian groups, as well as bases, weapons, and protection to the Mujahedin-e-Khalq, a group that opposes the current Iranian regime. The Iraqi regime has not attempted an anti-Western terrorist attack since its failed plot to assassinate former President Bush in 1993 in Kuwait. Instead, the regime has been very active in silencing dissidents abroad through intimidation, assassination, and imprisonment of the relatives of dissidents as hostages.

- Syria has continued to provide a safe haven and support to several terrorist groups, most of which oppose the Middle East peace negotiations with Israel.
- At the end of 2000 Libya was attempting to mend its international image following its surrender in 1999 of two Libyan suspects for trial in the Pan Am 103 bombing. (In early 2001, one of the suspects was convicted of murder. The judges in the case found that he acted "in furtherance of the purposes of . . . Libyan Intelligence Services.")
- Cuba has continued to provide a safe haven to several terrorists and U.S. fugitives and maintained ties to state sponsors of terrorism and Latin American insurgents. Colombia's two largest terrorist organizations, the Revolutionary Armed Forces of Colombia and the National Liberation Army, both maintain a permanent presence on the island.
- North Korea harbors several hijackers of a Japanese Airlines flight to North Korea in the 1970s and maintains links to other terrorist groups. The Philippine government recently declared that the Moro Islamic Liberation Front had purchased weapons from North Korea with funds provided by Middle East sources.
- Sudan continues to serve as a safe haven for members of al Qaeda, the Lebanese Hizballah, al Gama'a al Islamiyya, Egyptian Islamic Jihad, the Palestinian Islamic Jihad, and Hamas, in spite of pious pledges to help the United States combat terrorism.

Why wasn't the Taliban of Afghanistan on that list? This is where reality parts company with diplomacy. Afghanistan was not listed as a state that sponsors terrorism because the U.S. State Department did not recognize the Taliban as the government of a state. At the time of this listing, Afghanistan had no official government and therefore could not be a state that sponsored terrorism. It is the kind of distinction one expects from diplomats.[18]

State-sponsored terrorists have enormous advantages over the homegrown kinds. The former receive training, equipment, safe haven, money, and intelligence from the sponsoring government. When members of a terrorist group strike, the harboring government often defends them. The sponsor makes angry demands for proof of the victim's outrageous accusations . . . proof "that will hold up in a court of law!" When you see this happen, you may reasonably assume that the protesting government knows perfectly well who committed the atrocity because it supplied and trained the men who carried it out.

It is important to note that *all* the official state sponsors of terrorism listed above are known to possess chemical and biological weapons.

International Terror

We come at last to the special case of the al Qaeda terror network, founded by Saudi expatriate Osama bin Laden.[19] Al Qaeda represents a special threat to residents of the United States because it has unique features that more traditional terrorist organizations don't share. Experts have described it as having the resources of a government without any of the responsibility, which makes this group hard to fight.[20]

- Al Qaeda is an umbrella organization providing a single point of contact for multiple militant groups. Through these member groups, al Qaeda receives support from multiple sponsor nations. Naturally, this support is very deniable.
- Al Qaeda is not associated with any specific nation but has about 700 core members from many countries and thousands of supporters all over the world. Osama bin Laden's personal bodyguard (60 men) includes soldiers

from Saudi Arabia, Yemen, the United Arab Emirates, Egypt, Morocco, Algeria, Jordan, Sudan, Pakistan, and Afghanistan. The network has training bases in Africa and the Middle East, and safe houses in many countries, including the United States.

- Al Qaeda is very wealthy and very generous. One journalist called it "the Ford Foundation for terrorists." In the first month following the 9/11 attacks, the United States and allied governments froze more than $24 million in Taliban and al Qaeda assets. Experts predict the number will go much higher. The profits from the Taliban–al Qaeda opium business are estimated at $50 million per year.

Osama bin Laden (center), Ayman al Zawahiri (right), and Mohamed Atef (left)[21] during their television appearance on October 7, 2001. Bin Laden praised God for the September 11 terrorist attacks and swore America "will never dream of security" until "the infidel's armies leave the land of Muhammad." (AP Photo/Al Jazeera)

- Al Qaeda has many of the qualities of a cult: communal living, charismatic leaders, and an extreme religious creed. Its leaders have twisted their faith to make killing innocent people a virtue, as with many cults before them.
- The U.S. press says these terrorists are "willing" to die for their cause. This is not correct. The terrifying thing about al Qaeda's soldiers is that they are *eager* to die for the cause because the act expiates all their sins. Imagine that you have been taught from childhood that you are a Sinful Soul and will spend Eternity Burning in Hell. But wait! There is One Path to Salvation for the Truly Faithful. Wouldn't you be eager to sacrifice yourself too? Our strategic thinking has not caught up with this grim new reality.
- Al Qaeda's noble goal is to drive U.S. forces (and civilians) out of Saudi Arabia, home of the Islamic holy sites of Mecca and Medina. Part of this goal is to overthrow the current Saudi government, with which bin Laden has personal issues. On a grand scale, al Qaeda is dedicated to uniting all Islamic nations into one empire under a new caliph, signifying a return to the ancient glory of Islam. It is an ambition calculated to unite zealots of multiple races and nations, who normally could not agree on the color of an orange.
- The hated enemy is the United States, as the sponsor of the "Jewish Crusader" invaders of Palestine. In this Al Qaeda members see themselves as resistance fighters who will never give up until the invaders are driven into the sea. Wherever Moslems are oppressed, al Qaeda soldiers appear in the role of resistance fighters. They cynically claim Somalia (anti-U.S.), Bosnia (anti-Serb), and Afghanistan (anti-Soviet) as their greatest "victories," so far.
- The United States is an easy scapegoat because Western lifestyles and attitudes conflict so starkly with Islamic

fundamentalism. This is an excuse, of course, but it can be used to motivate the bitterly envious masses. Our best qualities (e.g., religious freedom and tolerance) are abominations to fundamentalist Islamics.

• There are reports that al Qaeda has its own laboratory for chemical and biological weapon development and further rumors that it has been bombed and destroyed in a U.S. air strike.[22] It doesn't matter. Al Qaeda certainly has both the finances to create its own weapons and the network connections to purchase a barrel of anthrax when it needs one.

Because al Qaeda is an umbrella organization, its leadership does not depend on one man. Bin Laden founded the network, but his top lieutenants are famous leaders in their own right.

• Dr. Ayman al Zawahiri, the founder of the Egyptian Islamic Jihad, is often identified as the number two man in al Qaeda. Al Zawahiri is justly famous as the mastermind behind the 1981 assassination of Nobel Prize winner and president of Egypt, Anwar Sadat.
• Al Qaeda's head of military operations is Mohamed Atef. Atef established the al Qaeda network in east Africa and recruited the men who later carried out the embassy bombings there. According to statements by Tony Blair, prime minister of Great Britain, Atef planned the September 11, 2001, attacks on the World Trade Center and the Pentagon.[23, 24]
• The head of the Taliban, Mullah Mohamed Omar, is a grim figure, always dressed in black, who never allows himself to be photographed. His right eye, lost to Soviet shrapnel, is stitched shut. He is a famous resistance fighter and a religious cult leader in his own right, as well as having been the de facto head of the state of Afghanistan before the 9/11 attacks.

If Robin Hood goes down under an airstrike, Little John and Friar Tuck will step over his body and assume command. Al Qaeda is not a snake; it is a hydra. Cut off one head and two will grow back.

So what happens if I send this book to press and a week later the leaders of al Qaeda are all rounded up and shot? Was it a waste of effort? I don't think so. The evil genie is out of the bottle, and nothing will put it back. As long as Israel exists, Arab resistance fighters will try to destroy it. As long as the United States supports Israel, militant splinter groups will use this nation as a convenient scapegoat. The more bombs and missiles we expend on terrorist camps in the Middle East, the more determined the survivors will be to revenge themselves on us. If we can crush al Qaeda, their multinational fighters will just reappear elsewhere under another name and keep going. We haven't seen anything yet.

We need to do some long-range planning. The next step is to explore the ways that terrorists might attack us and discover what defenses exist against them.

CHAPTER 3

WEAPONS OF TERROR

Now that we know the terrorist game plan, it is time to look at their tools. What weapons can they bring to bear on our cities and homes? What are the effects of those weapons? How do we mitigate those effects?

Lone terrorists are limited in their weapon selection by their isolation, their poverty, and the fact that they'd really rather stay alive. Anybody can make a pipe bomb in the basement, throw a Molotov cocktail, or blow up a chlorine tank car on a railroad siding. For that matter, anybody can hijack an airplane. The lone lunatic can do a lot of damage.

Organized terror groups, such as cults and resistance groups, are large, wealthy, and connected. Biological and chemical terror is within their reach on the do-it-yourself basis. For instance, in 1991 the FBI broke up a plot by the Minnesota Patriots Council to poison IRS officials using ricin, a deadly toxin extracted from common castor beans members of the group ordered through the mail.

International terrorists have access to any weapon you can name. Their sponsor countries have stockpiles of chemical and biological weapons and are trying to create or obtain nuclear weapons. What little they don't have, they are working hard to get. The terrorists have access to these weapons through their sponsors and friends of friends across the terror network.

"WORST-CASE" DAMAGE ESTIMATES

In this section I occasionally quote authoritative estimates of the number of people who would be killed in various types of terrorist attacks. *I* did not make up these figures, but they *are* made up. "Worst-case" estimates are deliberately inflated figures used for planning purposes. The press frequently picks up worst-case numbers and treats them as predictions, which is very misleading.

I'll give you an example. Suppose two jetliners were to crash into the Twin Towers of the World Trade Center and knock down both buildings? What would be the casualty estimate for this unlikely calamity?

An emergency services planner would construct the estimate using worst-case assumptions. First we assume the largest possible jetliners, carrying holiday loads of travelers. That would be two Boeing 747-400 airliners carrying 540 passengers and crew members each. Now we assume that every office in the towers is in use and all occupants are present, including 1,000 janitors. That's 25,500 people in each tower. We assume that the jets crash into the base of each tower, cutting off escape, so no one gets out alive. Cut off at the base, the towers fall over in opposite directions, smashing a dozen nearby buildings. Each secondary building is presumed to contain 3,000 people and 100 janitors. The wreckage spills into the streets, burying the equivalent of 25 city blocks of sidewalks. The number of pedestrians killed per block is estimated at 2,500 based on the reported density of crowds at last year's St. Patrick's Day parade, because terrorists like to strike on holidays. In all, the attack could kill or severely injure *151,780* people! The real World Trade Center attack killed just under 3,000 people, as you know. Be careful when people offer you their worst-case casualty estimates. They can be instructive, but they are usually overblown.

DIRECT ATTACK

A direct attack uses firearms and explosives to kill people and destroy property. This is most of what we have seen so far, including the attacks on September 11. In the past, this type of attack involved shooting up a crowd of strangers at a train station or airport or leaving a bomb at a post office. In recent years, it is more usual for the terrorists to deploy a van full of explosives, with or without a suicide bomber. The 9/11 attack was this same model scaled up to include 19 suicide agents and multiple flying bombs. Even a nuclear explosion falls into this category. It would be bigger but not different.

What is the attraction of direct attack? The explosions, fire, and smoke create dramatic visual images. The heroic rescue efforts keep the story alive for at least a week. For terrorist organizations, this is like taking out prime-time advertisements telling the world of their issues, their plans, and their achievements. They get recruits and donations from the glorious news coverage.

How hard is it to put together a car bomb? The classic formula is a few bags of a certain kind of fertilizer, a few gallons of kerosene, and a blasting cap. After the Oklahoma City bombing, authorities have made a renewed effort to prevent bomb-making materials from falling into the "wrong hands." There is no comfort in this. Explosives are available

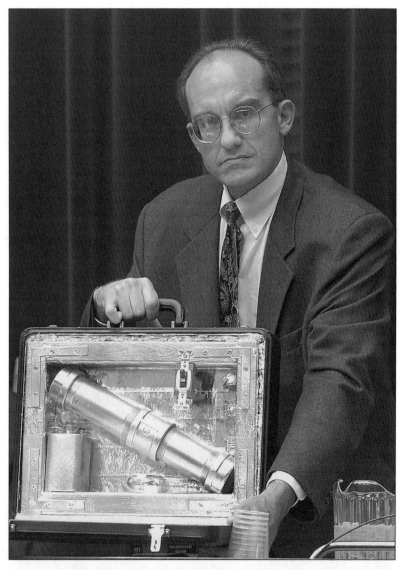

House Armed Services Committee staff member Peter Pry displays a model of a Russian nuclear suitcase bomb, October 26, 1999.[1] The Russians say about 100 such bombs are missing. (AP Photo/Dennis Cook.)

all across this country for construction, road building, mining, oil well drilling, and building demolition. People who can plan and execute a four-airliner suicide attack can certainly burgle a warehouse and get all the explosives they need. They don't have to smuggle them into the country or make them from scratch. (Shortly after the 9/11 disaster, 700 pounds of explosives used in oil drilling were stolen from a company near Houston, Texas. It's not difficult.)

Is there any chance that the terrorists would come directly after you, personally? Most of us would laugh at the idea, but I have a friend in Los Angeles who doesn't laugh. He once made disparaging remarks about Ayatollah Khomeni (dictator of Iran at that time) to a local television crew. The remarks were aired on the evening news as local color. Later that night, someone drove by and shot at his home with an automatic weapon.

The terrorists aren't all at a comfortable distance. Some of them live right down the street.

CHEMICAL WEAPONS

When you think of chemical weapons, think of insecticides for people. Some of the weapons are intended to incapacitate only; others offer immediate death. From the point of view of this book, we'd like to know how likely we are to see each of these chemical agents in the field, how much warning we might get, and whether or not we can tell which areas are contaminated and which are not.

We should be careful not to focus too tightly on "official" chemical weapons when we think about terrorists. In 1984, the Union Carbide Corporation had a little leak of methyl isocyanate from a plant in Bhopal, India. The accident killed 3,800 people and partly disabled another 2,680. Hand-held antitank rockets, or any shaped charges, can blow a hole in just about any storage tank you might want to name.

Placard Numbers and Evacuation Distance

In the paragraphs that follow, I have included the U.S. Department of Transportation (DOT) hazardous materials (Hazmat) placard number of each substance and the initial downwind evacuation distance in case of a major "spill." The placard number is interesting because it tells you what is inside a railroad tank car or a tank truck. Gasoline, for instance, is placard number 1203.[2]

The initial evacuation distances should be evaluated with caution. I have cited the initial downwind distances recommended by DOT for a "large spill at night," which is its worst case. These figures rarely exceed 10 miles and are intended for the initial evacuation only. Authorities expand the evacuation area as they get more information about where the toxic plume is blowing. I have included this information because it is useful to compare one distance with another as a rough indicator of toxicity. (If the recommended evacuation zone is 5.0 miles, you are *not* safe at 5.1 miles.)

Nerve Agents

Nerve agents are almost exactly the same thing as the insecticides you use in your garden (the carbamates and organophosphates). In fact, some of the nerve agents were discovered by chemists trying to invent new insecticides.

Nerve agents make it impossible for nerve cells to transmit impulses. The details are fascinating to the biochemist, but the net effect is that nerves just stop working. When the agent is inhaled as a vapor (in sufficient concentration), the victim suffers eye, nose, and lung irritation; pupil contraction; and air hunger (tightness in the chest, gasping for air). The victim passes out in convulsions in about a minute. Paralysis makes it impossible to breathe, and the victim dies.

When the poisoning occurs through skin contact, nothing happens for a few minutes. Then there may be muscular twitching, sweating, nausea, vomiting, and diarrhea.

Depending on the exposure, the victim may quickly collapse, go into convulsions, and stop breathing.

From all the talk of nerve agents in the news, you will recognize these five agents: tabun (GA), sarin (GB), soman (GD), GF, and VX.[3] The two-letter designations are the North Atlantic Treaty Organization (NATO) military designations for the agents. The agents in the "G" series allegedly were given the code letter G because they originated in Germany; the "V" allegedly stands for venomous. GF and VX have no common names.

TABLE 1

Nerve Agent	Hazmat Placard Number	Initial Evacuation Distance (large spill at night, in miles)
Tabun (GA)	2810	1.9
Sarin (GB)	2810	7.0+
Soman (GD)	2810	6.5
GF	2,810	3.2
VX	2810	0.6

All these substances have the same placard number, 2810. In fact, there are quite a number of chemicals that use this placard, and none of them is friendly when spilled.

The nerve agents are not "gases," technically, but liquids at room temperature like water or alcohol. Droplets of these liquids on the skin are deadly; the drops evaporate into an equally deadly vapor in the space of a few minutes. In the open, the vapor dissipates after a while, leaving no permanent contamination. Some nerve agents have a faint smell;

others don't. As a weapon, the poison is usually associated with an explosion that scatters the drops and vapor over a wide area. Protective equipment must cover the entire body and provide a safe air supply. Getting *out* of the protective suit requires assistance from a decontamination team. The standard nerve gas antidote is atropine, itself a poison in large doses, injected intramuscularly in 2-milligram increments. Soldiers in combat carry injection kits, which are not available to the general public.[4]

One would guess that domestic terrorists don't have access to nerve gas, but sometimes they surprise you. The Aum Shinrikyo fanatics in Japan released sarin on two occasions. The first time, they gassed residents of an apartment building, killing seven and injuring about 200. On the second occasion, they released sarin on five crowded subway trains, killing 13 people and injuring several hundred. They made their own sarin, not in a basement but in a fully equipped chemistry lab.

Do state-sponsored terrorists have access to nerve gas? The nerve agents can be manufactured in insecticide factories. All nations use insecticides, and since many nations make their own, there is no way to prevent them from making some nerve gas on the side. The United Stares bombed an alleged nerve gas factory in Sudan, a sponsor of Islamic terrorism, during the Clinton administration. Iraq manufactured and used tabun against Iranian troops in the 1980s. The sponsoring states know how to make chemical weapons, they have stockpiles, and they use them. Why would they refuse to share with their clients?

A typical gas shell or bomb cannot contaminate a whole city. A true nerve gas attack will probably be a fairly small one and utilize an enclosed space such as a subway, tunnel, theater, or aircraft for maximum effect.

Vesicants

The classic vesicant is mustard gas (sulfur mustard, H or HD). It has been available to the world's armies since World War I. Vesicants burn the eyes and skin and produce horrible blisters. If you breathe mustard vapor, the damage happens inside your lungs. Lewisite and phosgene oxime are also vesicants and are more effective but less common than sulfur mustard.[5]

TABLE 2

Vesicant	Hazmat Placard Number	Initial Evacuation Distance (large spill at night, in miles)
Mustard gas (sulfur mustard, H, HD)	2810	0.2
Lewisite	2810	1.1
Phosgene oxime	2811	1.9

Mustard "gas" is delivered by explosion as droplets of a yellowish, oily liquid that does not evaporate significantly until it becomes warm. The droplets are therefore persistent and dangerous for hours or days on exposed surfaces and for weeks to years in sheltered locations. Exposed to hot sunlight, the droplets evaporate into a vapor, which smells like mustard, onion, or garlic. This vapor is heavier than air and tends to flow along the ground, which is perfect for trench warfare.

The lethal dose of mustard, applied as a liquid to the skin, is more than a teaspoon of oil painted over about 25 percent of the victim's body. This is a *large* dose, which explains why very few World War I mustard victims died.

The vapor, however, is more dangerous, especially to the lungs and airways. The classic attack involves spraying the droplets around at night. The droplets evaporate in the hot sun the next morning, suddenly filling the air with deadly vapor. The delayed effect takes people by surprise.

To move around in a mustard-contaminated area you need whole-body protection and a safe air supply. It is sobering to note that after 80 years of research, there is still no antidote to the effects of mustard. On the other hand, horrible and painful as it is, mustard injury is not usually lethal.

Everyone who has a chemical weapons stockpile has mustard gas. Iraq used mustard bombs against Iran during their 1980–1988 war, causing tens of thousands of casualties. Once again, one gas bomb doesn't affect a very large area, and smuggling a large supply of mustard gas into the United States won't be easy. A mustard attack will probably be a small one.

Corrosive Gases

In terms of chemical weapons, the classic corrosive gases are chlorine and its relative phosgene. In a broader sense, inflammation of the lungs and airways can be caused by many kinds of chemicals.[6, 7]

TABLE 3

Corrosive Gas	Hazmat Placard Number	Initial Evacuation Distance (large spill at night, in miles)
Chlorine	1017	4.2
Phosgene	1076	6.9

Chlorine is a dense, acrid, pungent, greenish yellow gas that is easily recognized by both color and odor. We have all smelled chlorine in tap water, swimming pools, and laundry bleach. You can smell it at concentrations that are not dangerous, which offers some warning. By accident I once got a strong whiff of chlorine in a chemistry lab: it was like being punched in the nose, and my sense of smell was seared and never recovered. Phosgene is a white cloud that hugs the ground and smells like new-mown hay. If you can smell it, you are in trouble.

In either case, getting caught in the visible cloud means immediate death simply because the gas displaces all breathable air. You can't drive a car through a green cloud of chlorine because there isn't enough oxygen to keep the engine running. The engine just dies—and so does the driver.

Chlorine and phosgene burn the airways and lungs. The pain is intense, and the victims panic and run for their lives. For those who have been exposed and seem unharmed, it may slowly get worse over the following few hours, but many recover completely with no long-term effects. Severe cases die of pulmonary edema (like severe asthma) and choking on fluid coughed out of the lungs. Medical treatment helps, but there is no actual antidote to the chemical injury.

Historical note: Adolf Hitler was a gas attack victim in World War I. It made such an impact on him that he never allowed poison gas to be used on the battlefield in World War II, even when it was clear that Germany was losing. He did use a chlorine derivative (Zyklon B) in the gas chambers of his death camps, however.

Protective equipment? Some gas masks will filter out chlorine and phosgene for a limited time, but to walk through that green cloud you need self-contained breathing apparatus (SCBA, which is scuba gear for firefighters). A filter mask does not supply oxygen.

Can the terrorists get chlorine and phosgene? The good news is that chlorine and phosgene are not popular as modern weapons of war. We probably won't see them used on the field of battle, even in the Middle East. The bad news is that chlorine is the seventh most abundant industrial chemical in the United States. It is shipped around the country in railroad tank cars that contain up to 90 *tons* of chlorine gas. If the car is ruptured because of a train wreck or a terrorist explosion, the chlorine cloud can spread downwind for miles. You can find these tank cars parked on railroad sidings beside large municipal water or sewage treatment plants. Look for 1017 on the placard.

It doesn't take a rocket scientist to attack an unguarded tank car. You don't have to be a cultist. You don't have to bring a bomb. All you do is climb up and open the valve. (But how long can you hold your breath?)

As for phosgene, it is one of the heat decomposition products of carbon tetrachloride (placard 1846), another extremely common industrial chemical.

Cyanide

Cyanide is a simple compound of carbon and nitrogen that stops cellular respiration like a silver bullet. Cyanide victims often have bright red blood in both veins and arteries because the surrounding tissue cannot absorb oxygen from the blood. Hydrogen cyanide and cyanogen chloride are the two principal cyanide weapons because they can be deployed as gases.[8]

TABLE 4

Source of Cyanide	Hazmat Placard Number	Initial Evacuation Distance (large spill at night, in miles)
Hydrogen cyanide (AC)	1051	2.4
Cyanogen chloride (CK)	1589	5.0

The French deployed hydrogen cyanide against German troops in 1915 and 1916, but it was not very effective. The gas is lighter than air and quickly rises out of the kill zone. The French tried again later with cyanogen chloride, which contains cyanide and chlorine and is heavier than air. This was more effective. There are reports of cyanide bombs being used in the 1980s in the Iran–Iraq war and in Iraq's attempt to exterminate the Kurds.[9]

Hydrogen cyanide is a colorless or pale blue liquid or gas. It has the classic odor of bitter almonds, but many people are unable to smell it. Cyanogen chloride is a colorless gas with a highly "irritating" odor, according to the literature. The first symptoms of moderate cyanide poisoning are rapid, deep breathing and shortness of breath. The victim may show excitement, anxiety, personality changes, and agitation progressing to seizures. Heavy sweating, flushing, weakness, and vertigo may also be present. These early symptoms are followed by convulsions, loss of consciousness, and respiration failure. In cases of severe cyanide poisoning this parade of symptoms does not have time to develop. Death intervenes almost instantly.

There are medical antidotes to cyanide poisoning that are fairly effective. These are chemicals such as amyl nitrate and sodium thiosulfate that are administered intravenously. *These are not home remedies.*

Cyanide is readily available in the United States as an industrial chemical in plastics, photographic development, fumigation, metallurgy, and many other processes. The terrorists can purchase, steal, hijack, or blow up a cyanide shipment anywhere in the country.

How would they use it? A cyanide bomb exploded at the Super Bowl game would be big news but wouldn't cause as many casualties as you might think. Hydrogen cyanide floats up into the sky. Cyanogen chloride sinks down and pools on the ground. Neither weapon directly targets the thousands of spectators in the stands. It is more sobering to contemplate the same quantity of cyanide gas released into the ventilation system of a skyscraper, or in the Holland Tunnel in New York City. Note again that these attacks would be on a small scale, comparatively speaking, with limited casualties. Terrorists are not going to murder half a city with cyanide.

Incapacitating Agents

Incapacitating agents are chemicals that make the victim confused and delirious. Examples would be LSD, atropine, and scopolamine.[10] Aum Shinrikyo planned to spray people with LSD as part of its Armageddon vision, but the opportunity never materialized. In the 1950s, the Central Intelligence Agency experimented with incapacitating agents as part of its MKULTRA mind-control research.[11]

In 1959, at the height of the Cold War, someone put powdered atropine into the saltshakers of the Voice of America cafeteria in Munich that served more than a thousand employees. The plot was discovered just in time. The dose of atropine that would have been sprinkled on an average meal would have rendered the victim delusional for hours. It had exactly this effect on a military lab technician who, when ordered to run a toxin analysis on the salt, *tasted* it.[12]

BIOLOGICAL WEAPONS

Biological weapons are living agents, usually bacteria or viruses, that cause disease in the targeted population. Some bioweapons are very deadly, while still being relatively easy and inexpensive to make. Countries known to have biological weapons and to be sponsors of terrorism include Iran, Iraq, Libya, and North Korea. At the time of the Kuwait invasion, Iraq had both aircraft bombs and Scud missile warheads loaded with biological weapons.[13] The only thing that keeps Iraqi biological weapons out of terrorist hands is Saddam Hussein's deep and abiding love for the American people.

There have been lone fanatics who have tried the biological route. Larry Wayne Harris achieved his moment of fame when the FBI arrested him for claiming he had military anthrax, while he was still on probation for fraudulently obtaining samples of plague bacillus. Aum Shinrikyo mounted seven biological attacks in Japan, four with anthrax and three with botulinum toxin. At the time of this writing, the United States was coming to grips with anthrax letters sent to prominent people in government and the news media. Compared with what is possible, biological terrorism to this point has been remarkably ineffective. We cannot count on that trend to continue, however.

Aerosol Particle Size

It is important to know what an aerosol is and why particle size is so important.

An aerosol is a suspension of fine particles or droplets in the air. The particles are so small that they do not readily settle to the ground. Smoke and fog are familiar, visible aerosols. Finely dispersed aerosols can be completely invisible and undetectable.

To be an effective vehicle for a chemical or biological weapon, the aerosol particles need to be from 1 to 5 microns in size.[14] (A micron is a thousandth of a millimeter.) It happens that this particle size is perfect for sticking to the lining of your lungs. Smaller particles just float in and out of your lungs and don't stick. Larger particles get caught in the mucus membranes of the nose and pharynx and never reach the lungs.

One to five microns is a very fine powder indeed.

People who should know better are on the news telling us that anthrax particles this size indicate sophisticated and expensive technique, out of reach of homegrown terror. It is true that you need expensive industrial equipment to create a few tons of anthrax aerosol with good stabilization, highly uniform particle size, and other characteristics of a reliable, mass-produced product. It is *not* true that a private individual cannot generate a rough-and-dirty sample containing aerosol-sized particles in his home workshop. The sample would be small and have an inefficient mix of particle sizes, but dumped into a subway ventilation system it would be very dangerous.[15]

That discussion is all academic, however. There are nations unfriendly to the United States who have the industrial equipment to make as much weaponized aerosol as they want and have been doing so for years. These nations sponsor terrorist groups. If a terror organization wants a jar of anthrax powder—or a truckload or a bomb—all it has to do is ask for it.

Biosafety Levels

One indication of the relative danger posed by various biological weapons is their official "biosafety level" designation.[16] Microbiologists classify disease organisms into four groups, each of which requires different safety precautions.[17] This system gives us an idea of how dangerous an organism is when we hear about it in the news.

- *Biosafety level 1* applies to agents that do not ordinarily cause human disease, such as *Lactobacillus* spp., which makes milk turn sour. No special precautions are needed beyond basic neatness, sanitation of surfaces, lab coats, rubber gloves, and hand washing.
- *Biosafety level 2* is appropriate for agents that can cause human disease but whose potential for transmission is

limited. An example is *Closteridium tetani*, which infects wounds and causes tetanus. Procedures are performed in a vented isolation cabinet; the air must pass through a high-efficiency, particle-arresting (HEPA) filter before being recirculated. Otherwise level 2 is only a little more strict than level 1.

- *Biosafety level 3* applies to agents that cause serious human or animal disease and may be transmitted by the respiratory route but do not ordinarily spread by casual contact. Lab workers can be protected by vaccination or medical treatment. An example is the rabies virus. The lab has a dedicated ventilation system that keeps the air pressure lower than in the surrounding rooms. All vents and vacuum lines have HEPA filters; water lines have backflow valves. There is a separate changing room where researchers change in and out of dedicated lab clothing, including head covers and respiratory protection. After use, the dirty clothing is baked in an autoclave before being laundered. This is much more strict than level 2.

- *Biosafety level 4* is used for exotic agents that pose a high risk to life, which may be transmitted by the aerosol route or casual contact, and for which there is no vaccine or therapy, such as the Marburg virus. This is the "space ship" laboratory. It is completely sealed and has an airlock with interlocking doors that cannot both be open at the same time. Windows are sealed and made of unbreakable glass. Changing rooms include chemical showers. Personnel wear positive-pressure spacesuits. Exhaust air from the lab passes through *two* HEPA filters before being discharged outside. Activities are monitored on closed-circuit TV so there will be a record if anything goes wrong.

Biowar organisms tend to be levels 3 and 4.

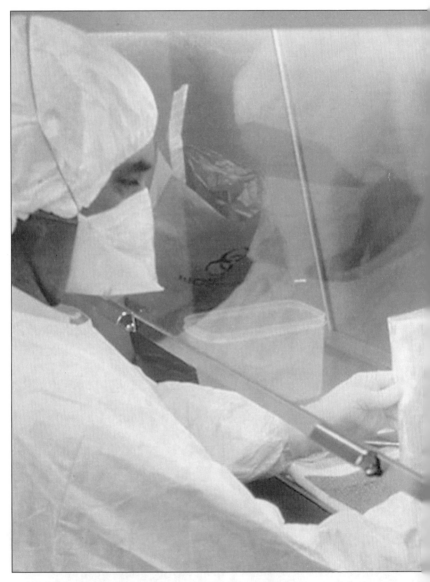

A scientist at Wadsworth Center laboratory in Albany, New York, handles suspected anthrax in a biosafety level 3 laboratory. This is the only correct way to open an anthrax letter. (AP Photo/New York State Department of Health.)

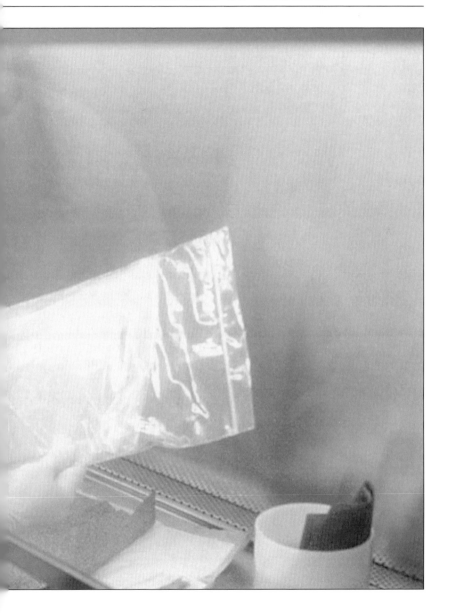

Anthrax

When I first drafted this section, it began with this sentence: "Anthrax is the bioweapon that terrorists are most likely to use." A week later the news was full of anthrax-laden letters sent to newspapers, TV personalities, and politicians. Compared to what is possible, the anthrax letters were crude and amateurish.[18, 19]

Anthrax is terribly effective, cheap to make, and easy to use, provided that you can solve the aerosol problem. It also has a long incubation period, which means the attackers can be long gone before public health officials detect the attack.[20-23]

Anthrax (*Bacillus anthracis*, biosafety level 3) is a bacterial disease of cattle and livestock that can be deliberately inflicted on humans by dusting them with freeze-dried, powdered anthrax spores or by spraying them with tiny droplets of a liquid preparation. The spores are deadly at concentrations that cannot be seen or smelled, and they float right into buildings on the ambient air. There is no such thing as an automatic anthrax alarm.[24] The bacteria can be cultured in vats using agar gelatin mixed with sheep's blood.

The bacilli naturally form spores that are extremely hardy in the environment. Nobody really knows how long anthrax spores can remain viable in soil, but it is "decades" at a minimum. There is some thought that the bacteria can actually *live* in the soil. In California, anthrax is endemic (occurs naturally) in 28 areas in the Salinas Valley, the Central Valley, and the Owens Valley.[25] It is common wherever cattle and sheep graze.

Anthrax has been responsible for several famous epidemics in history with great loss of human life, but these epidemics will not be repeated in the modern United States. Anthrax hides in the soil, lying dormant for years until a flood or drought washes (or dusts) forage plants with spores. Livestock ingest the spores with the fodder and

ANTHRAX LETTERS

How do you recognize an anthrax letter? The example letters and packages displayed by the FBI look like they were assembled by sloppy and illiterate children with greasy hands. Even the stamps are crooked and mis-aligned. Look twice at anything that just isn't *right*.[18, 19]

What if you receive an anthrax letter in the mail? The correct answer is to set it down gently, walk away, and call for professional help. Wash your hands with soap and warm water immediately. Meet the first responders on the sidewalk and brief them. The first responders will want to clear the building and keep everyone together until public health authorities arrive. They'll wear SCBA if they enter the building.

It is tempting to think that you could install a HEPA isolation cabinet in your mailroom so that an anthrax letter would not contaminate the building. The isolation box has some merit if you *always* open *all* letters and packages inside the cabinet, but that just isn't practical. Of course, you could use the isolation cabinet for all suspicious-looking items, to see if they are really anthrax letters or just ordinary *letter bombs*.

Set it down. Walk away. Call for help. Don't be stupid.

quickly sicken. Once started, an anthrax epidemic among livestock can be self-sustaining because the organism is present in excrement and dead carcasses. Flies visit the excrement and the carrion, and then land on forage plants and regurgitate fluid on the leaves (fly spots). Healthy animals eat the newly contaminated plants, and the cycle is repeated. The only solution is to quarantine the animals and burn or bury the carcasses.

In ancient times, however, people didn't understand what caused the epidemic. Imagine a struggling farmer near imperial Rome whose whole flock of sheep starts to die. The farmer thinks, "The animals are dying, so I'd better butcher them and sell the meat right away." The farmer develops black, open wounds on his skin, called eschars, from handling the infected meat. This *cutaneous anthrax* is ugly but generally not fatal. People who unknowingly eat the infected meat develop *gastrointestinal anthrax*, which is *very* ugly and always fatal if untreated. The farmer also skins the dead animals and sells the hides. Merchants who handle the skins inhale anthrax spores and develop *inhalational anthrax*. The death rate is virtually 100 percent for these unfortunates. These effects explain the historical anthrax epidemics. But the key lesson is that people don't catch anthrax from one another; humans catch the disease from infected animals and animal products.

In the case of inhalational anthrax, the inhaled spores don't actually attack the lungs. The spores are collected from the lungs by macrophages, which are white blood cells that engulf suspicious particles and carry them to lymph nodes to be destroyed. Within one to six days the anthrax spores germinate inside the macrophages and kill them. The patient becomes feverish and starts to feel chest pains over the next two to three days as the lymph nodes of the chest fill up with active anthrax bacilli. Once in the lymph nodes, the local production of toxins by anthrax bacilli causes swelling, bleeding, and necrotizing of tissue in the lymph nodes and other organs in the center of the chest. The bacilli can then spread to the blood, leading to septicemia and causing hemorrhagic meningitis in about half the patients. Shock, vascular collapse, and death follow within another 24 to 36 hours.

In the United States, inhalational anthrax is extremely rare, about one case in 10 years prior to the 2001 outbreak.

Few doctors have ever seen it. If terrorists can acquire a hundred pounds of anthrax spores, this will change suddenly and tragically. Imagine that it is a cool Monday afternoon in Los Angeles. Two men load a pair of heavy suitcases into the back of a rented private plane at the Torrance airport, southwest of the city center. The suitcases contain a hundred bags of anthrax powder, smuggled in from Iraq. They take off into a gentle northwesterly wind and fly northeast across the Los Angeles basin on a standard flight plan for Palm Springs. One man keeps the plane on course, doing nothing suspicious, while the other dispenses a tan-colored powder into the slipstream of the aircraft. An hour later, they load the empty suitcases into a rented car at the Palm Springs airport and drive away into the night.

Monday night, millions of Angelinos drive home after work. Everyone in the southeast half of the county goes to sleep with tiny anthrax spores floating in and out of their nostrils. The contaminated air blows softly across Irvine and Costa Mesa on its way toward El Centro, far to the south. The spores gradually settle to the ground.

Tuesday afternoon, a few people call their doctors complaining of flu-like symptoms. They get the usual advice. Drink plenty of fluids; get plenty of bed rest; call back tomorrow if you are not better.

By Wednesday quite a few people are calling their doctors. It looks like a new flu epidemic has hit town. A few dozen victims show up in emergency rooms in various hospitals. Some are sick enough to be admitted, and blood tests are done. Sometime Wednesday afternoon a careful pathologist spots the anthrax bacilli in a patient's blood sample. The first diagnosis of inhalational anthrax causes hasty tests to be run on other feverish patients. By midnight, specialists from the Centers for Disease Control and Prevention (CDC) and the U.S. military are flying toward

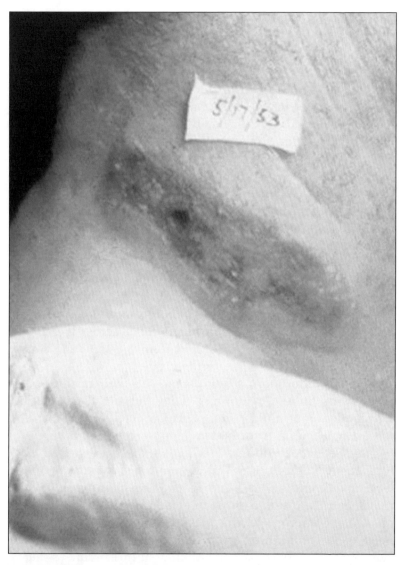

Cutaneous anthrax produces large black eschars on the skin. The cutaneous form is far less dangerous than the inhalational and gastrointestinal forms of the disease. (Courtesy of the Public Health Image Library, Centers for Disease Control and Prevention.)

Los Angeles, closely followed by CDC "push packs" containing tons of stockpiled antibiotics. On Thursday the first victims begin to die, and by Friday the biggest medical imperative is to collect and destroy the bodies before the corpses generate new spores. (You can't catch anthrax from a sick person, but you *can* catch it from a decaying corpse.) Police and firefighters go from door to door handing out antibiotics. The medication will help prevent the disease in the healthy, but it won't save the victims who are already visibly sick. Most of them will die.

The world watches it all on TV. The president circles over Los Angeles at 30,000 feet to show support.

Freeways out of Los Angeles are packed as people try to take their children out of the danger zone. There isn't much point in that by this time, but they don't understand that. Fresno, San Diego, Palm Springs, and other outlying population centers receive a flood of refugees. Many of these refugees subsequently become ill, but *the illness does not spread to local residents*. That's the only nice thing about anthrax.

How many victims might there be? In 1970 the World Health Organization (WHO) presented a scenario very similar to this one, in which 50 kilograms (110 pounds) of anthrax spores were released from an airplane upwind of a city of 5,000,000.[26] The WHO estimated 95,000 deaths plus another 125,000 incapacitated by illness, with a swath of victims extending more than 20 kilometers (13 miles) downwind of the release point. The exact figures can be manipulated by changing various assumptions about weather and medical care. The important point is the scale of the damage: an anthrax attack of this type could kill 10 times as many people as the collapse of the World Trade Center did, and the economic disruption would be unimaginable.

Protection? You can sort through these protective strategies, but keep in mind that terrorists never provide early warning of an attack. They are terrorists, not extortionists.

They like surprises.

- *Vaccine:* People in high-risk professions, such as veterinarians, can get anthrax vaccinations. That's really the only protection, and it isn't a very reliable vaccine. It needs frequent booster shots. It will be interesting to see whether this vaccine suddenly becomes more widely available to the public as our national understanding of terrorism matures.
- *Antibiotics:* If you have been exposed to the spores but don't have any symptoms yet, large doses of antibiotics can discourage the disease from developing. The CDC has a rapid-deployment cache of antibiotics for just this purpose, but in a surprise attack it will arrive too late to help the first victims.[27, 28]
- *Self-contained breathing apparatus:* SCBA provides real protection against inhalation injury, but the air tank is only good for half an hour.
- *Filter masks:* The spores are about 1 micron (mm) in size, which means you need a certified HEPA respirator to exclude them. A HEPA-certified filter must retain all particles as small as 0.3 micron in size at an efficiency rate of 99.97 percent.

The real trick is to put on the HEPA mask, or SCBA, before the airborne spores reach your location. That would be a few minutes after the attack, which could be three or four days before anyone knows about the danger. In practice, the mask isn't going to help.

As a reality check, some critics say that it is impossible for mere amateurs to create an effective anthrax aerosol, and they might be correct.[29] Bioterrorists have been remarkably ineffective with their attacks. On the other hand, the same critics might also conclude that it is impossible to demolish a 100-story skyscraper using only boxcutters.

Amateurs don't approach a problem the way traditional laboratory scientists do. For instance, while scientists were debating whether or not terrorists could learn to prepare their own anthrax cultures, the al Qaeda network simply purchased cultures from cash-hungry laboratories in Eastern Europe.[30] The issue wasn't about science; it was about scientists. Some scientists can be bribed—and Al Qaeda has quite a lot of money.

Tularemia

Tularemia, or rabbit fever, is normally a disease of wild animals, first isolated in Tulare County, California, but now known to be endemic to many parts of the world. It is a bacterial disease, *Francisella tularensis* (biosafety level 3), that can be employed as a biological weapon very similar to anthrax in use.[31, 32]

The important points to understand about tularemia are the following:

- *Like anthrax, tularemia is not contagious from human to human.* You catch it by handling the blood or meat of infected animals, or from spores deliberately sprayed into the air. (Of course, we might note that sick humans are also, technically, infected animals. Most of us don't handle their meat.)
- *In contrast to anthrax, tularemia is extremely virulent.* Ten bacilli are enough to give you the disease if they get into a break in your skin. Ten to fifty spores lodging in a lung are enough for infection. Lifting the lid of a culture dish to look inside creates sufficient exposure to catch the illness. The spores are fairly persistent in the environment on the order of weeks.
- *Compared with anthrax, tularemia is less deadly and easier to treat.* Untreated cases of typhoidal tularemia (the kind you get from aerosol exposure) have about a 35-percent mortality rate. Treated with antibiotics, the mortality rate falls sharply to 2 precent. The WHO study that estimat-

ed 90,000 dead from anthrax predicted only 30,000 deaths from a similar tularemia attack. (That study was done a *long* time before the CDC started stockpiling antidotes and antibiotics.)

There is a tularemia vaccine that provides protection against airborne spores, normally given only to laboratory researchers. Tetracycline given immediately after exposure can stop the infection from developing. HEPA or SCBA can temporarily keep the spores out of your lungs, but once again, in a surprise attack all of these measures will be days late. There is no sense breathing in the spores and *then* putting on the mask.

Do terrorists have access to tularemia powder? I cannot confirm that they do from the literature, but tularemia is one of the staples of biowar. Sooner or later there will be state-sponsored terrorists with access to this weapon.

Plague

Plague (*Yersinia pestis,* biosafety level 3) is one of the most famous of all diseases, mainly because of its role in the Black Death of the European medieval period. In the classic mode, rats and fleas carry the disease and sometimes transmit it to humans through flea bites. Most of these victims develop bubonic plague, in which the infection develops primarily in swollen lymph nodes (buboes) in the armpits and groin. Bubonic plague is not contagious, but about 10 percent of human victims develop pneumonic plague, which spreads rapidly from person to person by coughing.[33-36]

There have been three devastating pandemics of plague; the most recent one occurred only 100 years ago in San Francisco. From there the plague organism infected wild mammals (such as ground squirrels) and eventually spread throughout the western United States. We have a few human plague cases every year, mainly in Arizona and New Mexico.

Two recent pneumonic plague victims caught the disease

after being exposed to sick cats. A cat catches the disease by killing an infected rodent. As soon as the rodent's body starts to cool, the fleas jump off and go looking for the closest warm animal. They pass the disease to the cat by biting it. When an infected cat coughs, it sprays the plague bacilli into the air. The owner, or often the veterinarian, breathes in the droplets and catches plague. This misadventure happens about once a year in the southwestern United States and is often fatal for both cat and human.

We really have nothing to fear of a *natural* plague outbreak in the United States. Ecological and social conditions just aren't right for another Black Death pandemic in this part of the world. For one thing, somebody switched the rats. The Black Death was carried by the black rat *(Rattus rattus)*. Over the intervening centuries, the brown rat *(Rattus norvegicus)* has crowded out the black rat over much of its range.[37] The brown rat is not as comfortable living in human homes as its black cousin, which makes it a less effective plague vector.

On the other hand, plague is always included in the list of "possible" biowar weapons. Although plague is a bacterium, it has no dormant spore stage. It isn't easy to powder it and store it like anthrax. You have to spray *live* bacteria on people to infect them. The unprotected bacteria die quickly when sprayed into air and sunlight. This posed a challenge that was, regretfully, overcome by both the United States and the Soviet Union. Both sides (or at least Russia, since the Soviet Union no longer exists) have subsequently renounced this weapon and destroyed their stockpiles (they say), but the knowledge still exists.

For sake of discussion, let's assume that cultists have stolen the Russian secret formula for creating a plague aerosol and have sprayed it into the air in a major city. This would cause thousands of cases of primary pneumonic plague. The scenario develops along essentially the same lines as for anthrax, with a few key differences:

- *Unlike anthrax and tularemia, pneumonic plague is contagious from human to human.* This disease can spread through airborne droplets ejected by coughing. That sounds alarming, but medical personnel meet the threat by using surgical masks, gown, gloves, and eye protection. They don't have to don space suits.
- *Unlike anthrax and tularemia, plague aerosol deteriorates rapidly.* Plague bacilli live about an hour after being sprayed into the air. Sunshine is bad for them. Weaponized plague organisms, perhaps encapsulated in a gelatin coating, persist somewhat longer. This would be an important difference between an amateur attack and a professional bioweapon attack.
- *Plague aerosol produces primary pneumonic plague.* Pneumonic plague has a one- to six-day incubation period before the onset of fever with coughing and difficulty breathing. The patient may cough up frothy, blood-tinged sputum. Vomiting, abdominal pain, and diarrhea may occur. Patients survive about two days after the onset of symptoms and then succumb to severe, rapidly progressive pneumonia. If antibiotics are not started within 18 hours of the onset, mortality is virtually 100 percent.
- *Antibiotic prophylaxis and treatment are effective.* People who have been exposed to the aerosol can be given antibiotics immediately with a good chance of stopping the disease before it starts. Once the fever starts, antibiotics can save most victims if they are administered in time. That's the reason for the CDC "push packs" of antibiotics and antidotes.
- *There is a plague vaccine, but you can't get it.* U.S. military forces vaccinate military personnel against natural plague in parts of the world where it is common. The latest information is that the manufacture of this vaccine has been discontinued until a greater demand develops. It is for bubonic plague only and is not effective against pneumonic plague.

A famous World Health Organization (WHO) study estimated that 50 kilograms of *Yersinia pestis* sprayed over a city of 5,000,000 could create 150,000 cases of pneumonic plague and 36,000 deaths.[26]

What can you do to protect yourself? The first thing is to know that the attack is a brief event, not a continuous threat. There isn't much point in escaping after the fact: the organism is contagious and the infected zone will probably be placed under quarantine. Getting shot by the National Guard doesn't improve your survival quotient. If you are not an aerosol victim, wearing a surgical mask provides significant protection against becoming a secondary victim. You'll see just about everyone wearing the masks for a couple of weeks after the attack.

Do terrorists have this weapon? It is neither as easy to make nor as deadly as anthrax, so why would they bother? You could ask Larry Wayne Harris, who was arrested for illegally purchasing a freeze-dried *Y. pestis* culture.[38] He said he wanted to use it to create a vaccine to counter the threat of attack from Iran.

At its peak the Soviet biowar industry employed more than 32,000 people building plague weapons (and other things) at a site in Kazakhstan, which is now an independent Islamic republic. Its southern border is about 200 miles from Afghanistan. The project collapsed with the fall of the Soviet Union, and the project scientists mainly left the country to find jobs with pharmaceutical companies in the West. Some are known to have emigrated to Iraq and Iran instead.[39] Even if these two countries do not possess weaponized *Y. pestis* in their stockpiles, they certainly have friends who know how to make it.

Smallpox

Smallpox (*Orthopoxvirus variola*, biosafety level 4) is an

ancient enemy of mankind and the only one that we truly conquered and put behind us. Now it turns out that someone wants to bring it back. It is once again the Russians who bear the primary responsibility for this, and we have to wonder whether they succeeded in destroying all the smallpox bombs and warheads they made in the 1980s. Boris Yeltsin ordered the stockpile destroyed, but verification is always an issue.[40, 41] It turns out that Uzbekistan, at least, still has a stockpile of Soviet biological weapons on an island in the Aral Sea.[42]

Smallpox. (Courtesy of WHO.)

In the discussion of common biowar weapons, smallpox is the only one that is a disease of humans and humans only. Anthrax is a disease of livestock. Tularemia lives in rabbits and rodents. Plague is a rodent disease. Even the viral hemorrhagic fevers (discussed later in this chapter) normally live in animals. Smallpox is a human disease that spreads aggressively from one person to another and never appears in any other host.

Before the era of vaccination, virtually everyone caught smallpox sooner or later, and about a third of the victims died.[43] The mummies of some of the Egyptian pharaohs, including Ramses V, bear smallpox scars on their faces.[44] After 3,000 years there is still no treatment for it, but vaccination provides substantial protection. In 1980, the WHO declared smallpox extinct outside of laboratories, which was one of the golden achievements of modern public health efforts. Smallpox vaccination programs were discontinued throughout the world. We now know that the Soviets responded to this news by building a *huge* stockpile of smallpox bombs and missile warheads for use on the United States.[40] (Ronald Reagan didn't call them "the evil empire" for nothing.)

I don't believe we have much to fear from the Russians at the present time, but the disintegration of the Soviet bioweapons program left many Soviet microbiologists unemployed. People who know how to weaponize smallpox are now working for Iraq and Iran. State-sponsored terrorists might have access to this weapon. It is hard to imagine any way that lone fanatics or fringe groups could obtain it.

These are the important ideas about a smallpox attack on the United States:

- *Smallpox is deployed as an aerosol of virus particles that enter the body through the lungs.* The virus particles can retain their virulence for a long time outside the body, but the aerosol itself dissipates in a few hours.
- *Smallpox is a natural disease of humans.* It spreads from one person to another until aggressive vaccination and isolation stamp it out again.
- *A smallpox attack will place restrictions on travel.* There will be roadblocks and quarantine camps for people who try to flee. Expect a four-week quarantine.
- *There is no antiviral treatment for smallpox.* The only real "treatment" is vaccination. Routine vaccination of U.S. children was discontinued in 1973. Contrary to popular belief, vaccination immunity is not permanent, so older adults with vaccination scars are vulnerable, too. We are wide open to smallpox infection.
- *Emergency vaccine is available to contain an outbreak.* There is enough for one outbreak, anyway. The CDC has a few million doses of vaccine stockpiled, and there are another 100 million doses (or so) under the control of the WHO. The CDC has ordered 40 million doses of new vaccine but doesn't expect delivery until 2004.

- *Some people can't take the vaccine.* Smallpox vaccine is live *Orthopoxvirus vaccinia* virus, a cousin of variola. Vaccinia is well tolerated by most people (only biosafety level 2), but it attacks and often kills people who are immunodepressed, such as AIDS patients.[45]
- *The incubation period is 12 to 14 days.* The distinctive skin pustules don't appear until another two to three days later. At this point, the patient becomes contagious (mainly through coughing) and must be isolated until the pustules scab over and heal completely (i.e., all scabs fall off). The scabs contain live virus particles that retain their viability for years.
- *The standard quarantine period for smallpox is 17 days.*
- *The mortality rate is 30 percent for unvaccinated victims and 3 percent for vaccinated victims.* Vaccination after exposure offers some protection if done early.

We would suffer many casualties in a large smallpox attack. Many people will die, and the survivors would take weeks to recover. Economic disruption would be immense. Oddly, our best defense against this attack is the massive retaliation the world would visit on the perpetrators. Every nation in the world has benefited from the demise of smallpox, and only a few nations have the resources to bring it back. If the virus can be traced back to its source, I think the world's retribution would be truly biblical.

Ebola and Friends

In the past 25 years, there has been a great deal of research on the viral hemorrhagic fevers (VHFs, biosafety level 4). These are serious diseases with similar symptoms and histories even though many viral species are involved. You have heard of them as Ebola HF, Lassa fever, the hantavirus fevers, Marburg HF, yellow fever, dengue HF, Rift Valley fever, Argentine HF, Bolivian HF, Brazilian HF,

Venezuelan HF, Crimean–Congo HF, Kyasanur Forest disease, and Omsk HF.[46, 47]

These viruses live in animal populations and don't infect humans except by accident. In the case of Lassa fever, the accidents are pretty frequent. In West Africa, Lassa fever is associated with 10 to 15 percent of adult fever admissions to the hospital and perhaps 40 percent of nonsurgical deaths. When Lassa fever was first encountered about 30 years ago, it was a killer of doctors and nurses. Stringent barrier nursing (hair cover, mask, gown, gloves, foot cover, sharps precautions) has proven sufficient to control that problem.[48] At that time the source of the disease was a medical mystery, but it is now known that victims catch the disease from house mice, which scamper through food supplies, depositing virus particles through their urine and droppings.[49] This is similar to the situation with hantavirus in the U.S. Southwest.

Lassa fever, like other VHFs, does not spread by casual contact. Like AIDS, the virus is transmitted by exposure to a victim's bodily fluids, such as blood and semen. Infection through coughing is not common, and natural pandemics of VHF are considered unlikely. (See the section on genetically engineered diseases later in this chapter for an exception.)

The VHFs are extremely ugly diseases. The diseases differ in detail, but they all makes holes in capillaries, allowing blood to leak into surrounding tissue. As one doctor described it, "[the patient] literally melts in front of your eyes."[50]

An example occurred in 1988, when a Soviet biowar researcher named Nikolai Ustinov accidentally pricked his finger and infected himself with Marburg virus.[51] His colleagues made heroic efforts to save him, and he dutifully kept a journal of his symptoms as the disease progressed. On the fourth day he began to bleed under the skin. Later, he developed bloody vomit and diarrhea. Near the end, his body had become so porous to blood that it was seeping through the pores of his skin. According to a witness, he left bloody fingerprints on his journal pages. The blood, of course, was teeming with Marburg viruses. Ustinov's co-workers were very moved by his death. They didn't want his sacrifice to be in vain, so they salvaged as much virus as they could from his organs and used it to create new weapons. Ustinov lives on as Marburg virus, variant U. Some would say it is a fitting tribute.

The expected death rate from VHF diseases is hard to quantify because it varies from one disease to another and is very sensitive to the quality of supporting care and availability of antiviral medication. Also, the sample sizes (number of victims) for many VHFs are thankfully very small. This makes the statistics erratic. The following table will give you an idea of the mortality rates for various Ebola outbreaks.[52]

TABLE 4

Year	Ebola Species	Country	No. of Cases	Death Rate
1976	Ebola–Zaire	Zaire	318	88%
1976	Ebola–Sudan	Sudan	284	53%
1979	Ebola–Sudan	Sudan	34	65%
1994	Ebola–Zaire	Gabon	44	63%
1995	Ebola–Zaire	Democratic Republic of the Congo (formerly Zaire)	315	81%
1996	Ebola–Zaire	Gabon	37	57%
1996	Ebola–Zaire	Gabon	60	75%
2001	Ebola–Sudan	Uganda	425	53%

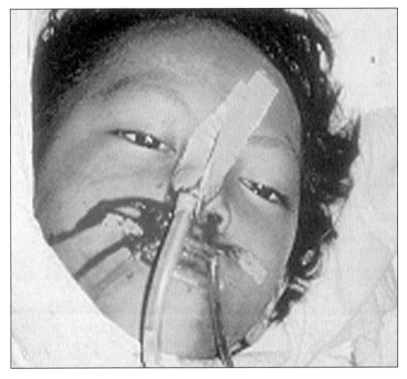

This little girl is a victim of dengue fever, one of the less dangerous VHFs. The patient bleeds steadily, and because the virus is in the blood, caretakers must use a barrier-nursing technique to avoid infection. (Courtesy of D.J. Gubler, Director, Division of Vector-Borne Infectious Diseases, CDC.)

There have also been "outbreaks" where one person caught the disease, received competent medical care, and lived—0 percent mortality. Overall, however, the VHFs have mortality rates closer to 10 to 15 percent. That's plenty bad enough.

Weaponized VHF is a dry aerosol, and people who breathe it are going to get very sick. With advance warning you can wear your HEPA respirator and get out of town.

(However, no sane person expects advance warning.) After the initial attack, VHF spread will be largely *nosocomial*, meaning that caretakers will catch the disease from cleaning up their bloody patients. Doctors and nurses know how to do that safely, but parents trying to nurse a sick child at home will be at extreme risk. If you are not handling a patient, there is little risk of secondary spread.

The incubation period for most VHFs is three to sixteen days. You should expect restrictions on travel out of the affected area, lasting a month or so. If you have been exposed to Ebola or Marburg, no one will want your tourist dollars.

Ribavirin is an antiviral medication routinely used against Lassa fever. It doesn't cure the disease, but it lowers the death rate. It seems to help with other VHFs, too, but opportunities to try it out are fortunately limited. Outbreaks of some of these diseases have been very rare.

Once again we come to the critical question: Could terrorists obtain this weapon? I have some really bad news for you.

You would think that a level-4 bioterror weapon would be technically beyond the reach of most terrorist groups unless they acquire it from a sponsoring government with a fully equipped viral weapons laboratory. Such governments and laboratories do exist, of course, but an organization like al Qaeda does not need them. It can do it by itself. All it needs is a sharp object like a safety pin.

As I write this chapter, the United States is actively bombing al Qaeda training camps in Afghanistan, where Osama bin Laden and his minions had (and may still have) their headquarters. For the past year, Afghanistan and neighboring countries have suffered an outbreak of Crimean–Congo hemorrhagic fever, one of the classic VHFs.[50] There could hardly be a worse development at a worse time in a worse place. A spoonful of blood from just one victim would be sufficient to fatally infect as many suicidal zealots as you could find. (Ustinov died from a pinprick.) Then you put the infected martyrs on airplanes to the United States. They probably could not get any kind of epidemic started, but the nation would come to a full stop until it was all sorted out.

Genetically Engineered Diseases

One of the former Soviet microbiologists says that his department succeeded in inventing a *new* virus combining some of the characteristics of smallpox with some of the characteristics of Ebola.[51] This sounds like science fiction, but unfortunately the techniques of genetic engineering have made it possible.

The usual thing is for the weapon scientists to breed new strains of bacteria that are resistant to the antibiotics we hope to use against them. For decades, the creation of antibiotic-resistant bacteria has been a standard technique of genetic research. This technology is easily adapted to weapons. For instance, there are credible rumors of plague and anthrax strains that are resistant to the usual antibiotics stockpiled by the CDC.[39] This may raise our casualty estimates somewhat, but it will not make a pandemic more likely. The rats and fleas just aren't going to cooperate.

One presumes that a combination of smallpox and Ebola would have Ebola's mortality rate combined with variola's contagiousness. That sounds like a big "improvement" over either disease alone. Perversely, if the hybrid disease kills people faster than smallpox does, it might actually be less dangerous than either parent disease. Smallpox is highly communicable because there is a long period when the patient is contagious. Ebola immobilizes and kills its victims fairly quickly. This cuts down on the opportunities for the disease to spread.

Genetic recombination has a bright side, too. In fact, the new tools of genetic research will revolutionize our health in just the next few years. One small thing will be the creation of special omnibus bacteria containing genes from multiple disease organisms. These bacteria will be used to create inexpensive, broadband vaccines. One inoculation could produce immunity to multiple diseases at once, and the designer vaccine would be easier and cheaper to produce than the separate vaccines. It sounds improbable, but in principle it's the same thing as a virus that's half smallpox and half Ebola.

TOXIN WEAPONS

A "toxin" is a poison created by (and extracted from) a living organism. Toxins themselves are nonliving biochemicals. There are about 400 known toxins, which can be extracted from bacteria, plants, shellfish, snakes, insects, spiders, fish, coral, plankton, frogs, algae, and fungi.[53] More are being discovered every year. As weapons, toxins are usually deployed as aerosols and should be thought of as chemical weapons. Toxins poison you; they don't infect you. You can't catch a toxin from another person. Generally speaking, toxins either paralyze the nervous system or destroy membrane tissue, producing bleeding. Some toxins make you very sick, but you recover. Some kill over a period of days. Some kill so quickly that, according to the Australian stonefish legend, you can take only seven steps before you collapse.

Botulinum Toxin

Although there are many types of toxins, relatively few are suitable for a large-scale attack on a city. Unfortunately, botulinum toxin is very well suited for this purpose. This is the toxin extracted from *Clostridium botulinum* (biosafety level 2), the species of bacteria that causes botulism food poisoning. It is so easy to culture that dozens of people poison themselves every year canning food at home. In terms of toxicity, botulinum toxin has the reputation of being, gram for gram, the most poisonous substance known to man.[54, 55]

Botulinum toxin is one of the staple biological weapons that all have in their stockpiles. Experts estimate that 8 kilograms (17.5 pounds) of toxin dispersed as an aerosol could kill half the people in an area of 100 square kilometers (40 square miles)—and make the other half very sick indeed. Botulinum toxin is very potent.

Victims unknowingly breathe the toxin powder into the lungs, where it lodges. The aerosol is invisible and has no odor or taste. There is no discomfort, and it takes a couple of days for the toxin molecules to work their way into the bloodstream. Once inside, the toxin binds *irreversibly* to motor nerve endings, rendering them useless. The toxin interferes with acetylcholine neurotransmitter production, effectively shutting down the motor nerves one cell at a time. This produces a kind of creeping paralysis that begins with difficulty seeing, speaking, and swallowing, and ends with respiratory failure a couple of days later. The patient's awareness and sensory nerves are not affected until very late in the process. Victims who do not die may be incapacitated for months.

There is an antitoxin that has reduced the death rate of accidental botulism to 10 percent, but antitoxin supplies are not abundant.

Generally speaking, the common means of disinfecting municipal drinking water are not effective for removing most types of toxins. There appears to be some scientific difference of opinion about whether municipal chlorination of drinking water is sufficient to destroy botulinum toxin. I expect these issues to be examined more intensively in the near future.

Ricin

Ricinus communis is the common castor bean plant, a 10-foot-tall bush with foot-wide purplish leaves. It is a native of Ethiopia that has spread like a weed throughout the temperate regions of the world. (I've seen it as a common roadside weed in Los Angeles.) It has poisonous seeds about the size of coffee beans. One seed can kill a child if ingested; four seeds are enough to kill an average adult. There are places where *Ricinus communis* is cultivated for the castor oil industry. Castor oil can be pressed from the seeds; the remaining mash contains a large concentration of ricin, a deadly toxin. The castor oil business generates hundreds of tons of ricin each year as a by-product. It is easy to build up a stockpile.[56]

The ricin molecule finds its way into living cells and binds to ribosomal RNA, which kills the cells by stopping protein synthesis. In the case of a biowar attack, the ricin would be delivered as an aerosol breathed into the lungs. It causes necrosis of the airways and alveoli, and the victim dies of hypoxia. Timing and mortality issues are hard to quantify because we haven't seen any aerosol ricin victims yet. The data are all based on lab animals.

It is possible to immunize a person against ricin or to deliver a timely dose of toxoid to stimulate antitoxin production, but this area of treatment appears to be more theoretical than practical in our context.

Toxins are molecules, a great deal smaller than bacterial spores and even viruses. Whether or not a HEPA respirator would filter out toxins depends on the size of the aerosol particles. The individual molecules are certainly small enough to pass through a HEPA filter, but particles that size don't usually lodge in the lungs.

As a weapon, ricin is a great deal less effective than botulinum toxin. Where 8 kilograms (17.6 pounds) of botulinum aerosol could decimate 100 square kilometers (40 square miles) of suburbia, it would take 8 *metric tons* (close to 9 tons) of ricin to achieve the same effect.[53] That's going to be a pain to smuggle through customs. For this reason, a ricin aerosol will probably involve a "small" target the size of a building, airplane, or subway station.

Additional Toxins

As I said, there are more than 400 known toxins. For the few that are suitable for weapons, the picture is generally the same in each case. The attack will be over before anyone knows it has happened. There might be a toxoid to use, but often there will be nothing, or not enough. The toxins have various poisonous effects, but at high doses they attack the lungs. It appears that there is only one thing the average family can do to protect against toxins: don't be there when it happens.

NUCLEAR WEAPONS

The "suitcase from Allah" is an idiom for a nuclear weapon in terrorist hands. It refers to 100 Soviet suitcase nuclear bombs that went missing at the end of the Cold War.[57] No one knows whether they were lost, destroyed, or stolen. One of these bombs could knock down a lot of buildings in New York City. The World Trade Center gives us only a glimpse of what a nuke might do.

The more combative Arab and Middle Eastern nations have struggled for decades to obtain their own nuclear weapons. Israel, Pakistan, and India have acquired their own nuclear capabilities. How long will it be before Iraq and Iran achieve theirs?

The hard way to acquire nuclear weapons is to create your own; that takes the resources of a government. The easy way is to steal one or buy it on the black market. There are nuclear warheads that fit into artillery shells, so size isn't an issue. Are we certain that nothing has leaked to the black market?

Here's a story that will put you in touch with the problem. Jamal Ahmed al Fadl is a Sudanese defector from al

Qaeda. He gave lengthy testimony at the embassy bombings trial in New York. His role in al Qaeda involved procuring property, food, and equipment for the organization. At one point he was asked to negotiate for a heavy shielded cylinder of black-market uranium for which al Qaeda was prepared to spend $1.5 million.[58] The cylinder he describes could as easily have contained a tactical nuclear warhead. Al Fadl says he doesn't know whether or not the deal was ever completed.[59, 60]

What are the effects of a tactical nuclear explosion? Let's assume that terrorists can detonate a 15-kiloton tactical nuclear device right at the foot of the Empire State Building.[61, 62] As tactical nukes go, this would be a fairly large one, comparable to the Hiroshima bomb.

Fifteen kilotons corresponds to a small tactical nuclear weapon, about the right size for terrorists to smuggle in. Detonated in a van at the curb, the explosion would demolish the bottom half of the Empire State Building, and then the upper half would come crashing down. The bomb would blast a crater into the bedrock and knock down all structures within a third of a mile. Beyond this distance, some buildings would collapse and others would be damaged out to about 0.7 miles. The blast would shatter windows out to 1.8 miles.

What about fires caused by the nuclear explosion? A tactical nuclear weapon explodes very quickly, emitting its thermal "flash" in about 1 second. (Maximum fireball radius is about 900 feet, or two-thirds the height of the Empire State Building.) Most of the fires started by the flash will be in the zone of total destruction and will be immediately extinguished by the blast wave. The burning material will be buried under tons of falling masonry. The wreckage will smolder for weeks, of course, just like at the World Trade Center.

Some of the buildings outside of the total destruction zone will catch fire due to blast damage. Everyone has seen the photos of the charred wreckage of Hiroshima. It is

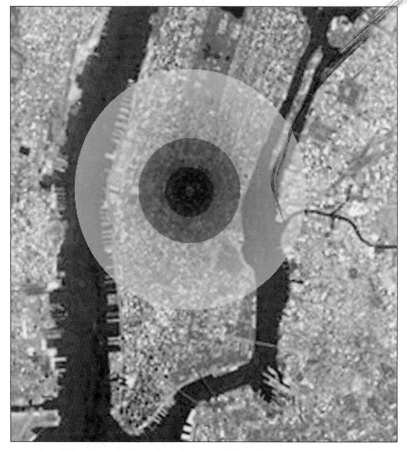

A 15-kiloton tactical nuclear device could make a serious hole in midtown Manhattan. Detonated at the foot of the Empire State Building, it would do the following:

- *Create a crater 200 feet in diameter (not shown)*
- *Destroy every building within 0.3 miles (central black region)*
- *Severely damage buildings within 0.7 miles (dark gray zone)*
- *Lightly damage buildings out to 1.8 miles (light gray zone)*
- *Deposit fallout in a swath for many miles downwind*

(Background satellite image courtesy of Spaceimaging.com.)

important to understand that the fires in Hiroshima spread from one building to another over the course of 24 hours. The buildings didn't just all turn black and collapse in an instant. There will be slowly spreading fires in the severe-damage zone because the streets will be blocked by wreckage and firefighters won't be able to reach the scene.

The total destruction zone runs from Park Avenue to Seventh Avenue, and the zone of severe damage reaches almost all the way across Manhattan Island from side to side. Notice also that the damaged area runs from Central Park on the north to Greenwich Village on the south. This means that most of New York City would still be standing, not to mention all the neighboring communities. Even so, it would be like having 100 World Trade Center bombings all at once. And the center of the rubble pile would be radioactive.

A ground-burst nuclear weapon expends a lot of its energy digging up the crater and does less actual damage than the same weapon exploded in the air. The seared rocks of the crater are made radioactive by the neutron burst during the instant of detonation, but New Yorkers will eventually solve that problem by just bulldozing rubble into the crater. Of more concern is the residual radiation from the fallout, which will spread for miles downwind.

The problem with ground bursts is that they loft tons of dirt into the radioactive mushroom cloud, where vaporized weapon residues "paint" the dirt with a film of highly radioactive metal. These dirt particles then "fall out" of the cloud as dust, mainly during the first few hours. The cloud doesn't sit still. It blows away downwind, with radioactive dirt sifting down.

The fallout particles are extremely radioactive right after the explosion, but the danger decays quite rapidly. Radiation exposure rates one hour after the detonation (when the first fallout hits the ground) decrease to 1/10th the original level within seven hours; 1/100th within two days; and 1/1,000th within two weeks. Fallout radiation has a short "half-life," meaning that it is very radioactive at first but the radiation fades away quickly.

What is the danger from the radiation? In the nuclear attack context, the danger is gamma radiation from the fallout particles. Gamma rays are practically the same thing as X-rays. They shine right through your body and do damage to the life process at the biochemical level. The body can repair most of this damage if given enough time, but an acute dose of radiation (too much in too few days) can be fatal. A person with acute radiation injury will feel dizzy and sick for a few days but will then recover and feel just fine for three or four weeks. After that, the victim deteriorates rapidly with symptoms rather similar to those caused by the viral hemorrhagic fevers. This is an injury, of course, not a communicable disease.

For a 15-kiloton ground burst, you should picture a dangerously radioactive zone about 10 miles wide and 50 miles long, extending downwind from the target. Radiation levels near the target will be much higher than farther away. Wind direction is obviously important, but weather statistics come to our assistance. For the most part, prevailing winds in the United States will deposit the fallout to the east of the target (somewhere between northeast and southeast for most cities). The cloud can blow in other directions, of course; this is just the usual case.

If you are caught in the fallout zone, your choices are to hide in a fallout shelter or run for it. In a terrorist attack the fallout zone will not be as widespread as in a nuclear war. At first, your emergency management authorities will advise you to seek shelter and stay there while they figure out where the fallout landed and how radioactive it is. Basements and subway stations are obvious shelters, but the middle floors of high-rise buildings also provide excellent protection from fallout radiation. Sit in the central hallway a few floors up from the street and a few floors down from the roof. Radiation protection there is excellent.

In a short time, probably within two days, the authorities will tell you to evacuate by driving north or south out of the fallout zone. Radiation levels decay a lot in two days, and half an hour spent driving to a clear zone is usually a good investment. Emergency managers are actually rather good at calculating the optimal moment to evacuate a fallout zone. (I used to teach people how to do this as a radiological defense instructor. My nuclear war survival books, *Life After Doomsday* and *Fallout Survival,* describe these subjects in much greater detail.)[63]

This scenario would kill about 40,000 New Yorkers in the first few minutes and a few thousand more in the radiation zone.[64] There would be many, many injured people, too, forcing evacuation of casualties to outlying communities for medical care. That's something we didn't experience with the World Trade Center bombing. The collapse of the buildings killed many but injured few.

Having described this catastrophe in such detail, I now have to tell you that I am not very concerned about its happening. I don't worry about a nuclear explosion on U.S. soil for several reasons. The first is that certain dangerous nations like Iraq and Iran have worked so hard to obtain a nuclear capability that they will hoard it. Once Saddam Hussein gets his fingers around a nuclear warhead, nothing will make him let go. The *threat* of the weapon is much more useful than the blast of the weapon. It makes him one of the nuclear big boys. Hussein's first nuke will go on his trophy shelf, and no one will dare touch it.

The second reason I'm not worried about a terrorist nuclear attack on the United States is that Hussein and his soul mates in the Islamic right wing would much rather use the bomb on Israel than on the United States. Iraq's Scud missiles can reach Tel Aviv, as we know, so the first nuke from Iraq would hit there. Then the Israelis would hit back with their own nuclear stockpile, and we'd all become involved in World War III.

The third reason I don't worry about a nuclear bomb on U.S. soil is that smuggling the bomb into this country runs great risks. The United States has highway sensors and aircraft that detect hidden or lost radioactive cargos, so there is substantial risk of the weapon's being detected and intercepted. The terrorists could put the bomb on a ship, of course, and detonate it in New York harbor. If they do, it will cut the casualties and damage roughly in half, because there aren't any buildings sitting out there in the water. (Don't be concerned about generating a tsunami in the harbor. Shallow-water nuclear explosions create disappointing waves.)

It is close to impossible for an independent lunatic, small cult, or most resistance movements to obtain a nuclear bomb. It strains credibility that Middle Eastern terrorists could build one of their own. It is possible, unfortunately, that they could obtain one by other means: those missing suitcase bombs will haunt us. We can't just assume that this is an imaginary threat.

Protection from a tactical nuke? If you live within a mile of ground zero, it should be clear that there is no protection. Farther away than two miles, it won't kill you outright but you could be injured. Downwind, it is possible for a family in a private home to build a fallout shelter and stock it for two weeks of occupancy. (See *Life After Doomsday* for ideas about plans.)

RADIOLOGICAL WEAPONS

There is one more nightmare to explore, and then we are done.

A terrorist radiological weapon is a trashcan full of powdered radioactive waste with a bundle of dynamite sticks buried in the middle. When it explodes, it creates a cloud of radioactive dust that contaminates the neighborhood. There are three aspects of this attack that generate concern.

- The first problem is that nuclear waste, unlike fallout from a nuclear explosion, does *not* decay rapidly. The contaminants have very long half-lives, and the radiation levels take years to die down rather than days. You can't just leave it around. You have to clean it up.
- Second, the dust shouldn't be washed away because that just puts the radioactive material into the sewers. Eventually it winds up in rivers and in the surrounding environments. You have to collect it. In a city, teams of people in protective clothing and respirators will do most of the cleanup by hand. Radiation exposure will have to be carefully monitored. Emergency services personnel from all over the country will fly in to contribute their measured two hours of time on the scene. In a rural landscape, it is a little easier to clean up the mess because you can bulldoze the top few inches of soil and cart it away to a nuclear waste site.
- Third, the victims who inhale the powder will be injured by it. Although we can't know in advance what material the terrorists would choose for their contaminant, uranium oxide is a good candidate. Uranium oxide particles lodged in the lung emit alpha radiation, which is especially bad for lungs. Tissue touching the particle receives a very high radiation dose that can damage or kill adjacent cells and cause the formation of fibromas. Think of it as scarring the inside of the lung. There is also significant long-term risk of lung cancer. Heavily exposed victims would likely die of lung damage over months.[65] The dust would be a source of continuing public health concern for years. That's why it has to be cleaned up.

The trashcan radiological bomb would be a tragic event and the cleanup would be expensive, but uranium is extremely heavy and even an automobile can't carry very much of it. The incident would be relatively small in terms of casualties and contaminated territory—on the order of the World Trade Center attack.

Unfortunately, terrorists might be able to scale up the attack as easily as hijacking another airliner and crashing it into a nuclear power plant. This scenario might bring about permanent changes in the American landscape. I say "might" because it is very difficult to assess the threat level of this possibility.

Like many Americans, I would like to have more electricity for my computers and air conditioners. I have spent years studying the effects of nuclear weapons, and in contrast to nuclear *war* the health risks of nuclear *power* just don't impress me. On the other hand, the September 11 terrorists have forced a paradigm shift in our thinking. (They changed the rules.) Before the attacks, the idea of a jumbo jet crashing into a nuclear reactor was far-fetched; the experts would laugh if you expressed any concern about it. Now we know that it could happen. In fact, it is not too much to imagine two or three jets crashing into the same reactor in rapid succession. Although the plants were designed to be hard to breach, it isn't really clear how bad the damage could be. At the time of writing, the Nuclear Regulatory Commission had just admitted that nuclear power plants were never designed to withstand these tactics.[66]

So we fall back on the worst case again. Suppose the attack causes a core breach and a partial meltdown. If Chernobyl is any example, such an event could contaminate an area the size of several counties.[67] In Russia, there are radiation-contaminated landscapes that have been fenced off indefinitely. In some areas, the Soviets built dams and canals to contain the runoff water from these areas, to keep radioac-

A view of the "ghost town" of Solnechny, 20 kilometers from the Chernobyl nuclear power plant, which was the site of a catastrophe on April 26, 1986. Since that time Solnechny and many other nearby towns have been completely abandoned. (ITAR-TASS photo/Viktor Tolochko.)

tive chemicals out of the local rivers. In Russia there are permanently abandoned towns in these quarantined areas.

Since we are speculating about what might be possible, let's look again at United Airlines Flight 93 on the morning of September 11, 2001. (Flight 93 was the one that was hijacked over Pennsylvania and turned back toward Washington, D.C.) The passengers fought with the hijackers, and the plane crashed.

The press speculates that this plane would have been used to attack Camp David, the White House, or the Capitol. I suspect it was aimed at the White House, but there is another disturbing possibility. The terrorists were amateur pilots, barely able to steer the jetliner. They were flying very low. The radar track of the hijacked plane looks to me as if they were visually following Interstate 73 to the southeast from Pittsburgh. The cockpit fight occurred near Somerset, Pennsylvania, and the plane crashed in a wooded field just a couple of miles north of the interstate.

The terrorists might have been on a magnetic course for the White House, which was only 135 miles to the southeast. On the other hand, they might have been following I-73 *visually*, as inexperienced pilots tend to do.[68] Near Somerset, the interstate curves to the northeast and leads to Harrisburg, 120 miles away. The Three Mile Island nuclear power plant is only 4 miles south of the freeway at Harrisburg. The big cooling towers are very visible on an island in the Susquehanna River. You just can't miss them from the air.

CHAPTER 4

TERROR TAKES AIM

At this point we have an idea of who the terrorists are. We understand the nature of the terror mechanism and the goals of the terrorist planner. We have examined their potential weapons. To evaluate our own risk, we need to know what targets the terrorists are likely to attack. By adding just a little imagination and common sense to our analysis, we can fill out a pretty reasonable target list.

SYMBOLISM, VICTIMS, IMPACT

How do terrorists pick their targets? Given a selection of appropriate targets, how do they decide which one is best? That depends on the type of terrorist.

I'll propose a simple formula for your consideration:

Target value = Casualties + Symbolic value + Practical impact

We cannot assign actual numbers to these terms, but the formula provides a convenient way to discuss the target selection process. "Target value" is the attractiveness of a target in the mind of the terrorist planner. This attractiveness is based on three factors:

- *Casualties* are important because they provoke retaliation and multiply the publicity value of the attack.
- *Symbolic value* means that the attack makes a political statement by attacking something that represents the true enemy. This is an attempt to play to the terrorist's audience.
- *Practical impact* means damage done to the enemy's military capability.

A target can be attractive because of casualties, symbolism, or military significance alone. It may also strike some kind of balance among all three factors. This makes perfect sense, but different types of terrorists select different types of targets. Why is that?

Lunatic Targeting
The lunatic loners attack symbolic targets and usually have little interest in mass casualties or practical impact. When I read interviews with Timothy McVeigh, I was struck by his bitter obsession with the federal government but his total lack of interest in the people he killed. The people were simply "collateral damage." He blew up the Alfred P. Murrah Federal Building in downtown Oklahoma City because it contained federal law enforcement *offices*. He wasn't after anyone in particular, and he didn't expect to have any practical impact on the FBI. The attack was purely symbolic.
Ted Kaczynski was a Luddite, violently opposed to the

march of technology and its impact on individuals. He struck back by sending letter bombs to engineers, scientists, aircraft manufacturers, and other individuals associated in his mind with technology. He didn't know any of these people. Hurting them didn't change anything. His bombs were designed to mutilate one person at a time. The targets were merely symbols of his imaginary enemy.

For both Kaczynski and McVeigh, casualties and military impact were not the issue. Their targeting formula was:

$$\text{Target value} = \text{Symbolic value}$$

The lesson we can draw here is that big symbols are likely to be big targets. Big symbols include famous buildings, famous institutions, and famous people. (Of late, there seems to be a bounty on famous news announcers, too.) As we have seen, sometimes the symbol has to do with the date of the attack, such as Millennium Year's Eve.

Fringe Targeting

What is the targeting policy of fringe groups such as animal-rights and antiabortion terrorists?

The special-interest fringe groups are trying to overthrow human nature and as such will ultimately fail. No one really has a lot of sympathy with lunatics who shoot doctors or people who commit arson to improve conditions for bobcats. These people see their special issues out of proportion to reality, and it makes their targeting very issue specific.

Most observers would say the fringe attacks are symbolic, done for publicity alone. If you read the reports, however, you get the disturbing feeling that the attackers thought they were doing something *practical*.[1] Blow up a clinic, save 1,000 babies. Kill a doctor, save 10,000 babies. Raid a research lab, liberate 1,000 pink-eyed white rats from slavery. (White rats released into the wild are like cotton candy for predators.) There is a sense of "somebody has to *do* something" in their exploits. Their operating formula is as follows:

Target value = Practical impact x Obsession

Fringe groups aren't attracted to either mass casualties or symbolic values. They want to "do something," and they try to go do it. Their obsession makes them overestimate the impact of their acts.

Cult Targeting

What about the religious cults? If we take Aum Shinrikyo as our model, it is clear that their victims were chosen at random. They wanted to create casualties for reasons that made sense in their mad cosmology but which the rest of us will never understand. Aum Shinrikyo wanted to kill lots of people, so they operated in the most populous city in the world, Tokyo.

Target value = Casualties

What is the lesson? When religious cults kill for religious reasons, they have no interest in symbolism or practical effect. They just want blood. In some situations, a dense crowd of people makes the perfect target. The more people, the more blood. Any dense pack of human bodies will attract their attention.

We can be a little more specific in the case of religious hate groups, such as the militant fundamentalist "Christian Identity" groups in the United States or the militant fundamentalist "Islamic" groups operating in the Middle East. These people don't just kill indiscriminately. They have target populations that serve as the focus of their hate, and naturally they prefer to attack the target group. Within that target group, however, subjects are usually chosen at random.

An example is the white supremacist who plants a bomb in a black church or an Islamic terrorist who throws a grenade into a Tel Aviv restaurant. We might note that religious cults have been known to commit casual murders of inconvenient people, such as defectors, opposing attorneys, police chiefs, and judges. That's plain old murder, not terrorism, but if you are an attorney it is important to remember. Some people actually *do* kill lawyers. Most of us just talk about it.

Targets of Resistance and Revolution
Resistance and revolution groups are a special case. The classic model involves isolated insurgents who provoke the government, gradually build support, become the champions of the people, and finally mount a revolution. Their targeting priorities shift as they evolve.

At first the insurgent group, lacking broad support, simply wants casualties. This forces the government to crack down on everyone, which broadens support for the terrorists.

Target value = Casualties

When the insurgents evolve into "champions of the oppressed," they shift their sights to such symbolic targets as government offices, police stations, and post offices.

Target value = Symbolism

Only in the terminal phase, full revolution, are they strong enough to seek out and destroy significant military targets.

Target value = Practical impact

A resistance group usually forms in response to an invasion and, oddly enough, goes through the same changes in target strategy but in the opposite sequence. At first members of the group are the remnants of the losing army, striking at practical targets like enemy outposts and patrols. This becomes too dangerous as the remnants weaken, so they shift to symbolic targets that don't shoot back. If peace breaks out, the last few fanatics may resort to bombs that create indiscriminate casualties, trying to reawaken the will to resist. You can see this happening in Northern Ireland, where the last remnants of the IRA are still setting off bombs while everyone else is at the peace table.

Targets of State-Sponsored Terrorism

State-sponsored terrorists are tools in the hands of their paymasters. The terrorists don't mind because they have a noble goal to pursue and, usually, an incumbent government to hate.

To analyze the targeting strategy of state-sponsored terrorists, you have to take into account the agenda of the sponsoring state. The Soviet Union supported insurgencies and, therefore, terrorists all over the world. The aim was ideological: to spread communism—and, incidentally, to broaden the sphere of Soviet trade. For instance, by fomenting and supporting insurgency in Cuba, the Soviets eventually established a military presence only 90 miles off the U.S. coastline and received massive sugar imports for making vodka. The goals of the sponsoring country were strategic. The Soviet Union didn't need to micromanage the Cuban revolution; all it needed to do was finance and equip the revolutionaries.

The state sponsors of Palestinian groups have much the same kind of agenda. "Here's the money; hurt Israel. We don't care how you do it." The terrorists choose their own targets to fit their own agendas.

The sponsoring state may have very specific military missions for their clients. Iraq has a perpetual conflict with its traditional enemy, Iran, in which these countries periodically go to war over the Shatt al Arab, a swamp on their mutual border. As part of this conflict, Iraq sponsors the Mujahedin-e Khalq (MEK), an Iranian resistance/revolutionary movement with a long history. In addition to other anti-Iranian activities, MEK is regularly involved in mortar attacks and hit-and-run raids on Iranian military, police, and government buildings near the Iran–Iraq border. Iraq receives the benefit of constant intelligence on Iran's military activities in this key area. The MEK terrorists serve as an intelligence arm of the Iraqi military.

On the other hand, sometimes the "state" cannot be viewed as a ponderous ideological bureaucracy but as a single man who has too little restraint and too much power. In this case the state-sponsored terror is really directed by one man, who may express personal animosities. Clearly this is what happened when Saddam Hussein ordered an attempt on the life of President Bush (Sr.) after the Gulf War.

Targets of International Terrorists

What is the targeting strategy of the militant Islamic right, whether it be al Qaeda or any of its kindred organizations?

The Palestinian organizations that fight a narrow battle against Israeli occupation behave like resistance groups. They create atrocities to provoke Israeli backlash. This keeps their ranks full while giving their soldiers something to do other than turn on their leaders. There isn't a lot that they can attack for the sake of symbolism, partly because Israeli security around high-value targets is very tight. As for attacking significant military targets, the Palestinians don't seem to be up to it.

The Islamic militants who attacked the World Trade Center and the Pentagon, however, had a very clear set of targeting criteria. They targeted symbolism. I have some doubt that the planners wanted massive casualties. They completely ignored practical military targets. Their targeting formula was:

Target value = Symbolic value + (some) Casualties

We know the terrorists targeted symbolism because the World Trade Center and the Pentagon were icons of U.S. power that people recognize all around the world. From this point of view, the fourth airplane was probably aimed for the White House, another important icon. The target planners wanted these famous buildings in flames for the publicity value of the news coverage. This is consistent with their earlier target selections, such as the various embassies in Africa and the abortive attempt to bomb the crowds at Times Square during the millennium celebration. These are all attacks directed against symbols.

As for casualties, it is not clear to me that the massive casualties inflicted at the World Trade Center were intended. Crashing a plane into each tower was sufficient to generate the desired publicity. The world saw the fires in New York and Washington and knew that the United States had been injured. I think the terrorist planner achieved complete success at that point, and the subsequent collapse of the towers surprised him.[2]

After the airplane crashes Americans felt shocked and helpless. We sat in front of our televisions and wrung our hands. We felt powerless in the face of these anonymous attacks. We didn't know what to say or do. Then the first tower collapsed, and horrified Americans rose out of their chairs and went to *war*. When the second tower collapsed half the civilized world stood up and joined us. In a real sense, the attack backfired.

Why did I say that the September 11, 2001, attack ignored military targets? They hit the Pentagon, but that's

Where do nuclear aircraft carriers dock when in port? I downloaded a 1996 satellite image of Norfolk, Virginia, and spent about an hour examining the shoreline until I found these carriers and two more nearby at Newport News. Mohammed Atta visited Norfolk just before the September 11 attacks. (Photo courtesy of TerraServer.com, Orbimage.com, and Aerial Images, Inc.)

just an office building that doesn't shoot back. Only 150 miles south of the Pentagon, at Hampton Roads, is one of the largest naval complexes in the world. That morning there were at least two Nimitz-class nuclear aircraft carriers tied up in port, the USS *Ronald Reagan* and the USS *Theodore Roosevelt*. Two more were at sea nearby, the USS *George Washington* and the USS *John F. Kennedy*. With good timing, the four-airliner attack might have damaged or sunk all four ships. That's $18 billion worth of ships, carrying 24,000 people and about 300 combat aircraft capable of attacking terrorist camps in the Middle East. Four fully equipped carriers contain 14 million gallons of aviation fuel and eight nuclear reactors. (Once again, worst-case estimates are inevitably *over*estimates, including this one.) Like the Three Mile Island cooling towers, you just can't miss an aircraft carrier from the air. The flight deck covers 4.5 *acres*.[3]

The terrorists aimed at the Pentagon instead of the carriers. Therefore, they were not interested in practical military targets. They were after symbolism and publicity, and they got it. Mohammed Atta, one of the September 11 hijackers, had visited Hampton Roads to examine exactly these carriers. He attacked the symbolic buildings instead.[4]

Bear in mind, however, that symbolism is in the eye of the beholder. Domestic terrorists are Americans, and they know their country very well. Islamic fundamentalists are quite ignorant of the United States, even when they are well educated. This is bound to interfere with their planning. Consider this item: In the Gulf War, Saddam Hussein tried to demoralize U.S. soldiers by saying that movie stars like *Bart Simpson* were seducing their girlfriends back home.[5]

In practice, this will lead them to misunderstand the practical importance of targets. For instance, they could blow up the White House and kill everyone in it, thinking it would decapitate our government and leave us without a leader. In reality, the nation would have a new president within the hour. Domestic terrorists understand that, but foreign ones do not. The new president would be really angry, too.

If We Were the Terrorists

What is the targeting formula used by U.S. military planners in this era of smart bombs and intelligent missiles? Our military emphasizes practical effect tempered by a fear of inflicting civilian casualties.

Target value = Practical impact – Casualties

The cost of our smart weapons has an impact on the planning. As President George W. Bush recently said, "I'm not going to fire a $2 million missile at a $10 empty tent and hit a camel in the butt." Therefore, our military would like to select targets that are worth more than the missiles and bombs are. Every civilian casualty is a political and moral liability, so our planners avoid civilian casualties as much as possible. This is exactly the opposite of the terrorist's target selection policy.

Americans are an ingenious people, and this makes us misunderstand terrorist targeting policy. It is trivially easy for the average American to think of ways to cause mass casualties in his land. Just ask your friends, "If you wanted to kill a lot of Americans, how would you do it?" The answers will keep you awake all night.

I'll give you one example. A terrorist has been sending letters with anthrax dust inside the envelope to prominent news organizations. The strategy hasn't been very effective. I asked a friend how he would improve on it. He thought for a minute and replied, "First I would find out who makes the return envelopes used by credit card billing services. Then I'd find out where the envelope makers get their glue. Then I'd use my ill-gotten millions to buy a glue company. I'd mix anthrax spores into envelope-flap glue. I'd contact the envelope makers and announce a sale on glue, undercutting the lowest prices of my competitors. Three months later, 90 million Americans would lick anthrax spores while paying their bills." He smiled and walked away.

We naturally assume that the terrorists hate us and are trying to kill as many Americans as possible. This leads us to anticipate attacks on the wrong types of targets. We can't predict *their* actions by thinking like *us*. We have to think like *them*, instead.

TARGETS NEAR YOU

To evaluate your personal danger, you need some idea of the likely terrorist targets in your area. Those could be symbolic targets, casualty targets, and possibly military targets. The emphasis depends on which group of terrorists you are worried about.

As an initial assessment of your personal danger, consider this quick test. On your way to work tomorrow open your eyes and look around. If you see more trees than cars, you can probably relax. If you see more cars than trees, you may have a problem. (From my office window I can see *thousands* of trees but zero cars.)

Symbolic Targets Near You

The first factor in the targeting equation is *symbolic value*. You probably can already name the large symbolic targets near your home and workplace. That may even be the reason you bought this book. On the other hand, many of us overlook the obvious. How would a terrorist planner view your town?

As a first cut, you should visit two or three pharmacies and family-style coffee shops near your home or place of business. Look for a rack of postcards, the kind that tourists mail home to their friends. The major icons of your community will be on display there. What pictures are on the postcards? Again, if the postcards show mainly rocks and trees, you have little to worry about. If they show large buildings, especially large *government* buildings, then you are in some danger.

You can extend this search to the Internet by opening up travel-related Web sites. At the time of this writing, a good example is www.lonelyplanet.com. This Web site (and many others) shows you maps of all the big cities in the United States, Great Britain, and Europe, with the iconic landmarks labeled in red. For instance, any description of New York City inevitably mentions the Empire State Building, the Chrysler Building, the Brooklyn Bridge, and the Statue of Liberty. If you browse a tourist guide to London, Big Ben and the adjacent Houses of Parliament just leap off the page. How could a terrorist not be attracted to these targets?

Perhaps the World Trade Center towers were targeted in part because they were huge phallic symbols of U.S. power. Or possibly the two identical towers just stood out on a postcard of the New York skyline. Or maybe they were just the tallest buildings in America. You might want to check the location of the country's remaining tallest skyscrapers to see how many are in your area.

Most people would immediately suspect that the Empire State Building is now the tallest building in New York, which is true. The Chrysler Building is the second tallest, and it is located only half a mile away. (You might think of them as the *fraternal* twin towers.) These two buildings are probably on everyone's short list of potential targets.

It is a little surprising to discover that most of our giant skyscrapers are actually in Chicago. That would be the Sears Tower, the Amoco Building, the John Hancock Center, the AT&T Corporate Center, and the Prudential Building (formerly the Guaranty Building).[6] How much symbolic value do they have? To a Middle Eastern terrorist planner, the destruction of any building with

"American" in its name will create good publicity. That would include both AT&T and Amoco.

You need to make a map showing the location of these landmarks in your area. We'll return to this map frequently to add targets and examine escape routes.

You don't usually hear of any type of terrorist attacking a state or local government building in the United States. Even the domestic terrorists focus on various branches of the federal government, according to their interests. You can sort by department, depending on which terrorist group worries you. For instance, domestic tax resistance groups inevitably focus on the Internal Revenue Service. If the militias ever get loose, they will target the Justice and Treasury Departments. Ecology terrorists might attack the U.S. Department of Agriculture or the U.S. Department of the Interior or perhaps the Environmental Protection Agency. Since these attacks will be small in scale, they will select outlying offices and federal buildings rather than the headquarters buildings in Washington, D.C.

The point is that there are no terrorist groups interested in attacking the Department of Commerce, the Veterans Administration, or the Department of Health and Human Services. It would be unreasonable to assume that *all* U.S. government agencies are in danger. Many agencies are so obscure that only their own employees know they exist.

Where do you find the list of U.S. government offices in your area? Look in your phone book under "U.S. Government." Pick out the sites that might attract terrorist attention and add them to your map.

Symbolic targets also include famous persons such as the presidents of multinational corporations and famous television personalities. Ted Kaczynski sent a letter bomb to the CEO of American Airlines. Tom Brokaw got an anthrax letter. Is there anyone in the world who has never heard of Bill Gates or Ted Turner? Ask yourself who is rich, famous, and powerful, and whether they have offices in your neighborhood? Look for the obvious. If you don't know about the Microsoft subsidiaries in your neighborhood, probably the terrorists don't know either. Mark the famous persons and their businesses on the map.

Casualty Potential Near You

The second major term of the targeting equation is *casualties*. Sometimes the bad guys just want to kill people. Often they don't or don't care either way. It is worth asking yourself how you might be caught in a mass-casualty attack. We are looking for something relatively simple that could kill or injure a large number of people, and you might be one of them. What comes to mind?

Even with chemical and biological weapons, it is hard to do much damage to people who are outside. The agents dissipate quickly, which means you usually need a lot of it to do a small amount of damage. Even with anthrax or botulinum toxin, you get more "bang for the buck" if you release the agent in a closed space. The traditional targets, mentioned in all the literature, are subway tunnels and large apartment/office buildings. Lately people have been wondering how effective this would be in a shopping mall.

Do you live or work in a high-rise building or some other structure with target value? How many people are typically in the building on a weekday? Is the building tall enough to make evacuation difficult? Are the exterior windows sealed shut? Basically, would the building be an effective *gas chamber?* If so, a gallon of sarin poured into an air-conditioner intake on the roof could do a lot of damage, and you could be caught in it.

It might be possible for really serious terrorists to attack an open-air neighborhood as described earlier using anthrax, botulinum toxin, or industrial chemicals. In my opinion, the

Three Mile Island nuclear power plant as it appears from a low-flying aircraft approaching from the west. This might have been the target of the fourth plane in the September 11, 2001, attack. (Courtesy of the Public Health Image Library, Centers for Disease Control and Prevention.)

low-hanging fruit here is in railroad tank cars. A shaped charge placed against the side of a chlorine car would force the evacuation of a large area and could easily create a few hundred casualties. Is there a railroad mainline near you? A freight yard? Mark it on the map.

The same hazard applies in varying degrees for any large tanks of chemicals. Is there an oil refinery near your neighborhood? (I grew up between two major refineries in Los Angeles, so the question resonates with me.) Is there a major water treatment plant or sewage treatment plant near you? If you are not sure, call your department of water and power. It probably has a Web site that explains why it has to put chlorine in your water. Are you near any major factories or chemical plants? Don't forget to include the nuclear power plants within 50 miles of your location. Mark everything on the map.

In 1985 Palestinian terrorists attacked the Italian cruise ship *Achille Lauro* in the Mediterranean Sea. A cruise ship is essentially a large floating hotel with the potential for both symbolic value and mass casualties. If the SS *United States* were still at sea, she would be a prime target for her name alone. I'm sure you can think of other cruise ships with politically symbolic names. Any one of them could supply a terrorist with publicity, magnified by the difficulty of getting wounded passengers to mainland hospitals. The news networks would agonize over the rescue operations for days.

Certain types of terrorists would be attracted to certain types of mass gatherings. We know that Islamic militants planned an attack on the crowd at Times Square on New Year's Eve 1999. Large, traditional parades such as the Rose Parade might fit this category. A presidential inauguration, the Super Bowl, the World Series, all present an opportunity to panic a crowd and cause casualties due to trampling. Do you live along the route of the Rose Parade? I have friends who do.

Military Targets Near You

It is my position that terrorists of whatever type don't usually attack significant military targets. On the other hand, the USS *Cole* had a very large hole blown in her side by terrorists in October 2000. I don't see this as a practical military attack, but rather a symbolic one like an embassy bombing.

Still, it seems so obvious that U.S. military personnel, equipment, and installations could become terrorist targets, either for their practical value or, more likely, for their symbolic value. The question is, would the terrorists know or care about the military targets near you?

First, do you know of any U.S. military installations near your home or workplace? The big ones are hard to miss. You can make a first cut by simply unfolding highway maps of your state and city and looking for federal sites. For instance, a map of Denver shows relatively few high-profile symbolic or practical targets until you notice the Rocky Mountain Arsenal out near Denver International Airport. We can envision a terrorist planner thinking, "Take off from the airport, turn west, crash into the arsenal. Looks good."

I don't want to belabor the obvious. Any military site you find is a potential target for various reasons, but is it a real one? Many military bases are vast expanses of sagebrush and dirt. If terrorists want to bomb dirt they can do it closer to home. Would the terrorist you have in mind want to hit this facility?

Finally, bear in mind that the really tiny military facilities just aren't on the radar scope. If you didn't know it was there, neither does the terrorist planner. He'll be looking at the big, famous targets, not the little, obscure ones.

Mark them on the map anyway. The rules might suddenly change

PART II

Protecting Your Family

Part II has to do with protecting your family. Now that we understand the terrorists, their weapons and targets, we can begin to assess your vulnerability and your response strategies.

For the most part, there are two kinds of survival strategies. One category involves moving out of the danger zone before, during, or after the attack. The second strategy is isolation: being able to close your doors and stay in a safe place for three or four weeks. Both strategies require preparation.

CHAPTER 5

SURVIVAL BASICS

What if the terrorists actually do strike your neighborhood? How can you protect your family and escape the effects of the attack?

In a few pages we will analyze various family escape strategies. These strategies focus on equipping your family to survive for a few days or week if you are either forced out of your house or locked up inside it by circumstances. The survival family has to be well equipped for self-sufficient living. What does that entail?

I once reviewed about 300 books on survival and self-sufficiency, so I can say with some authority that you can immerse yourself in survival lore. I have no intention of repeating all that information here when you can so easily purchase it elsewhere.[1] Instead, I'll give you the thumbnail course in family survival, based on 30 years' experience. The trick is to know what is important. That is not always obvious, however.

We are picturing a family of four with young children, trying to escape the effects of a terrorist attack. They may have to flee or camp out or go to a shelter or button up at home for days or weeks. What survival supplies do they need?

RULE OF THREES

Anyone thinking about survival should know the rule of threes. It is the expert's tool for establishing the priority of survival tasks when you are lost in the woods. I learned it from Ron Hood, the most savvy survival expert I know.[2] It goes like this:

- You can live three minutes without air.
- You can live three hours without shelter.
- You can live three days without water.
- You can live three weeks without food.
- You can live three months without love. But you won't like it.

These rules are deliberately somewhat silly to make them easier to remember. In the context of wilderness survival, the killer is shelter. Lost at night in the north woods, you can die of hypothermia in three hours. The rule of threes is your basic outline for all survival preparations. (The only thing it leaves out is sanitation, which is not much of a problem in the woods.)

SHELTER

In term of family survival preparations, the first priority is shelter. By this we mean the ability to keep the family *warm and dry* even though the weather is cold and wet.

- Facing the crisis in a snug, warm house is best.
- Surviving in a camper, trailer, or motor home is not bad, unless a tornado goes by.
- Sheltering the family in a tent is fine when the weather is nice but deteriorates rapidly in the rain and snow. Imagine two weeks in the tent, in the mud, with no chance to wash or dry out the bedding. Now imagine four weeks.
- You won't freeze in a Red Cross disaster shelter, but you won't enjoy it much.
- Camping without a tent in bad weather is inviting death from exposure. People have frozen to death huddled in cars.

You must be certain that you can keep yourself and your family warm in the worst weather you might encounter. Terrorists are not above timing their attacks to take advantage of bad weather.

If nuclear radiation is a factor in your emergency plans, you need to know a lot about *fallout shelters*, both the kind you construct in your back yard and the public kind in tunnels and large buildings. There are also books that can show you how to construct expedient fallout shelters designed at Oak Ridge National Laboratory 20 years ago.[3] These are remarkable designs field-tested by average families. Example plans are included as appendices to *Life After Doomsday*.

On the subject of emergency shelters, sometimes the fatal problem is being too warm, not too cold. Each person in your shelter (e.g., basement, car, tent, cabin, whatever) gives off as much heat as a 100-watt light bulb. For this reason, a crowded room will get very hot and stuffy. In an emergency, especially a fallout emergency, your shelter will be severely overcrowded. You must provide sufficient ventilation to create a cooling breeze or you will have to abandon the shelter prematurely.

WATER

In a survival situation people need a lot of water. In everyday life, a typical American "uses" about 80 gallons of water a day when cooking, bathing, laundry, sanitation, and landscaping are taken into account. Reduced to the absolute minimum, you can keep a prisoner alive on 1 quart of water a day under ideal conditions, which means cool weather, no exertion, and a carbohydrate diet. To provide a healthy amount of drinking water plus some for cooking, washing dishes, and bathing requires 2 gallons per person per day.

That doesn't sound like much, but each gallon weighs 8 pounds and takes up one jug of space. The jugs don't stack well. Jerry cans (5 gallons) are the largest containers it is practical to lift. For a family of four, a two-week supply of water would be 42 jerry cans, at 40 pounds per can, or 3/4 ton. It isn't going to fit in the trunk of your car, but you could put that many cans in your basement. I installed a 5,000-gallon water tank instead. It sits on the hill above my house.

If you are planning to relocate temporarily out of the threat zone, you will need to replenish your water supply on the road. You can count on towns outside of the threat area to share their water, but your survival preparations should include the ability to decontaminate surface water for drinking. Surface water in the United States is *not* safe to drink, so plan on purifying many gallons of water per day over a period of many days. Overdo it. Strive to provide more water than you think you need.[4]

For that matter, even if you hole up at home, your municipal water supply could be compromised. The water at the tap might not be safe to drink. The ability to purify tap water might be very important at some point.

SANITATION

We didn't mention sanitation under the rule of threes, but it has to be a part of your survival plan. If your plan is to stay home and you are confident of your water supply, then the toilets will keep flushing and you have no worries. If there is any reason to suspect that the water will be shut off or that you won't be near working toilets, then you need to provide alternative facilities.

Not being able to flush the toilet gets very old very fast. You learn to stretch your water ration to allow for flushing. Use pure water for drinking, bathing, brushing teeth, washing laundry by hand, cooking, and washing dishes. The dishwater, bathing water, and rinse water go into a bucket for flushing the toilet. If you dump the bucket suddenly into the bowl of the toilet it will flush just fine. You can only flush when the bucket is full, of course. That happens only once or twice a day.

If you have babies in diapers, you have a major problem. I know of only three solutions. One is to prepare to do a lot of laundry, possibly by hand. With babies in the family, you have to do that anyway. The second is to stockpile disposable diapers, a strategy that creates awkward storage and disposal problems, especially if you have to evacuate the site. The third solution is to pen the toddlers in the kitchen and let them run around without pants. Clean up after them like puppies. As I said, it is a *major* problem.

FOOD

Food is fairly inexpensive and easy to obtain in advance of the emergency, but you need to think a little about the kinds of foods you need to store.

If you plan to stay home during the crisis, the best emergency food supply is simply more of whatever you buy anyway. The old adage is "store what you eat and eat what you store." Canned goods can be stored for a year, sometimes longer, so it is easy to cycle the stockpile regularly. This is easy and very comfortable for the family. You won't have the challenge of feeding the children unfamiliar foods.

Canned goods are not the ideal solution if you need to pack two weeks of food into the car and drive away. Canned goods are heavy. Freeze-dried camping foods are easier to pack and prepare. Reconstituting dry meals requires additional water. Military MREs (meals, ready to eat) are available on the surplus market, but you should try a few before stocking up.

If you want to stock your home for *long-term* survival, you can purchase dried foods in bulk, packed under nitrogen in number 10 cans. Various companies offer these foods prepackaged in three-month, six-month, and one-year quantities.[1] I have had a closet full of these cans for 20 years. I can tell you that the stored food is just as appetizing now as it was when I bought it (you can read between the lines here).

The drawback is that these bulk-food programs are designed on the Mormon model and emphasize the bulk grains and beans more than the freeze-dried meats and vegetables. That's *whole-kernel* grain. You have to grind it into flour and bake bread. It takes special equipment and some practice. You will also want to store a lot of spices and flavorings that are not included in the bulk kit.

There are a lot of options for storable and portable food. The main issues are quantity (how many days for how many people) and quality (familiar, convenient foods or unfamiliar foods that are cheaper). Homemade whole-wheat bread is delicious, but it has a laxative effect on some people because of excessive bran. You need to experiment and find your own way here.

Nobody buys frozen survival food, except me. I have an

8-kilowatt generator to keep the freezer going, and in emergencies I survive on frozen pizzas, steaks, and ice cream bars. I got tired of reconstituted food a long time ago.

FUEL AND ENERGY

Fuel and energy are big issues in a survival program. Fuels tend to be expensive, bulky, and dangerous to store. When you run out of fuel, however, your survival options become remarkably narrow.

If you plan on bundling the family into the car and driving somewhere in an emergency, you need to confront the question of gasoline for the car. How far away is Grandma's house? How many gallons of gasoline is that? You can't count on the gas stations being open or having gas when you need it. If you store jerry cans of gasoline, you'd better do it safely. No sense blowing up your garage or setting fire to your house.

It takes quite a lot of energy to boil a pot of water. If you store two weeks' worth of freeze-dried dinners, how many propane bottles will you need for your camp stove? You get the idea. Nobody likes to munch dry noodles, but that may be your only option if you run out of fuel.

Part of your shelter plan is considering how to keep the house, motor home, cabin, or tent heated in the winter. What fuel will you use for heating? How much? If the electricity fails, does the furnace still run? (Mine doesn't, but I have a wood stove and two cords of seasoned oak outside.)

Energy also includes electricity. If your home or cabin loses electrical service, how much does that interfere with your survival plan? You may have your own well, but do you need power to run the pump? In much of the rural United States when the electricity goes out the water stops running.

Losing electric power doesn't mean that you are left in the dark, as long as you have planned for it. Make sure you have plenty of flashlights and batteries. Suppose you need to use your flashlight for two hours each night over the duration of the emergency. How many batteries is that? (There are new types of flashlights that use light-emitting diodes instead of traditional bulbs and are far easier on batteries than before.) You can also use candles or kerosene lanterns for nonelectric light. How many candles do you need for two weeks of evening light? You have to store the right amount of candles and also one or more fire extinguishers. In survival simulations children knock over candles rather often.

MEDICINE

The proper goal for emergency medical self-sufficiency is to be able to tell what is important and what is not. There are very reputable books on how to be your own doctor (sometimes) that teach you to cope with common emergencies and illnesses by yourself.[5] This is important if you are holed up in your basement while anthrax or nuclear fallout blows around outside.

Armed with a good book, you can approach your family physician about fortifying your medicine cabinet with the kinds of medications yachtsmen would stock on a long sea voyage. That way your doctor may be able to diagnose a condition over the phone and tell you what medicine to use. Be sure to get extra refills of your personal prescriptions.

What you *cannot* do is to stock up for a biowar attack on your family. It takes too many doses of too many kinds of medicines. The government has massive amounts of antibiotics and antidotes stockpiled, and its agencies really are ready to roll on a moment's notice. There is no need to compete with those programs.

I will be watching for public health authorities to open new immunization programs. When they start offering anthrax and smallpox vaccine, I'll be first in line.

If your family will be eating unfamiliar foods, you'll want

to stock up on medications that regulate intestinal activity. Your family will be frightened, which often hits the digestive tract. You'll also want a large supply of analgesics. Everybody will have a headache.

PERSONAL DEFENSE

The survival family needs to be armed, as all American families should be armed, but you don't need to go overboard. I speak as someone who has walked this whole path. I've been a combat artist all my life, including weapons training from one of the premier combat shooting schools in the world, the Gunsite Academy in Paulden, Arizona. I've played with all the guns and have met the experts eye to eye. To defend yourself, you need a gun that you can shoot skillfully, and you need to be *willing* to shoot it. The rest is just details.

Why? In this book we are talking about an average family trying to dodge a terrorist-created emergency. If you expect armed confrontations with other victims of the disaster, you are entertaining a common male fantasy. (Recognize it? It is the one where *your* shots always hit but *their* shots always miss. That's not reality.)

The terrorists are not going to come shoot at you, and neither are the neighbors. It is the universal experience of emergency managers that victims of a disaster pull together, treat each other like family, and risk their lives for total strangers. We all felt this reaction the day of the 9/11 disaster. You have heard the accounts of people carrying injured strangers down 40 flights of stairs to get them out of the burning buildings. You know about the firefighters who struggled up the same stairs and died to a man, trying to reach the desperate victims trapped on the upper floors. Heroism and altruism were everywhere.

Did you hear of anyone getting mugged on those stair-

This is Osama bin Laden's worst nightmare: women with weapons. This is the General Pistol class for women at the Gunsite Academy. (Photo courtesy of the Gunsite Academy.)

ways? Any robberies? Gang rapes? Assaults? Abductions? Drug sales? Pickpockets? Racial violence? You should be thinking, *Of course not!* That's right, and it wasn't just in the doomed stairwells. In the week following the attack, crime all over New York City dropped to *the lowest rate in 40 years.*[6] In disasters, people forget about their differences and show irrational love and cooperation for one another. It may not fit your preconceptions, but it is a fact. You can't afford to waste money on playing Rambo in the ruins. Assault weapons and ammunition are very expensive. For family survival, you need to spend that money on more practical supplies. The price of an assault rifle buys an awesome amount of food.

You won't need to defend yourself during a disaster. The subject doesn't come up. On the other hand, I believe that every responsible adult should be armed, and there is a basic kit. You should have a shotgun with a selection of shells suitable for hunting, pest control, and personal defense. There should be a pistol you can conceal on your person as your combat "first-aid kit," for those sudden emergencies when you are too far from the shotgun. Finally, there should be a rifle for those times when you need to reach out beyond conversational distances. Most of all, you have to embrace the unbending rules of firearm safety,[7] and you have to practice. Buying a pistol does not make you a gunfighter any more than buying a piano makes you a musician.

No reputable security expert will dispute that advice, but many will probably want to add to it. That's fine, but it's beyond the scope of this book.

THREE-DAY TEST

Survival families have a tradition called the "three-day test." Once you have your survival program set up, you simulate an emergency for three days and see how it goes. The test needs to be appropriate to the plan. Usually we at least shut off the electricity, heat, and water. We might make a rule that we can't use the telephone, go outside, or use the car or that we have to remain in the basement for the whole three days. Sometimes we *simulate* an electrical failure by sealing up the refrigerator and taping the light switches in the off position. You get to set up your own test to fit your program.

Whenever we do this, we find big holes in our plans. This is when you discover that you forgot to buy a nonelectric can opener. You'd really like to add a deck of cards to the kit. You discover you need *long* books to read out loud to the children. You overlooked a survival supply of dog food. You didn't save a stack of newspapers for pet sanitation. When your plan meets real life, the plan takes a beating. Take notes and be prepared to revise the plan.

I did this on a large scale once, as a county disaster coordinator. I invited 200 people to a spaghetti dinner at a meeting hall. After dinner a team of medical makeup experts went around the room pouring fake blood on everyone. Then we "crashed" a light plane into the middle of the building and turned out the lights. The first firefighters arrived seven minutes later. Within an hour we had 18 fire companies and six ambulances involved, with sheriff's deputies directing traffic and bloody bodies filling up the halls of the local hospital. I spent weeks writing up the results of the exercise. Compared with that, three days at home with the lights off is nothing.

You *must* test your plan. You need to confront the experience and learn from it.

CHAPTER 6

REDUCING YOUR RISK

To do a good job of assessing your personal risks and strategies, you have to understand that there is no such thing as safety. There is no such thing as security. There is only *relative risk*. As the head of a survival family, your job is risk management. There is no magic barrier to erect against hazard.

You probably bought this book expecting me to tell you the best kind of gas mask to buy, the right hazmat suit to wear, and which chemicals to stockpile for decontaminating your boots. That information is for people who are outside the contaminated zone and have a life-or-death reason to enter it, such as first responders.[1] This book is for people who want to keep their families alive instead. We're headed in the opposite direction, away from the threat.

It would be so simple if we could make a list of the "dangerous places" and never go there. But that's a good definition of paranoia. Instead, the idea is to arrange your life so that you minimize the amount of time you spend in the target zones. We have to do some serious thinking and realize that some of our naïve expectations about survival are likely to get us killed.

THE MYTH OF PROTECTION

In the next few pages we will evaluate a series of survival strategies to see how much protection they offer a typical family faced with a terrorist attack. It turns out that "protection" is a very misleading concept. We need to shed a few comfortable illusions before we proceed.

In professional emergency management, "protection" is a bad word that can get you into a lot of trouble. People expect "protection" to transform some horrifying danger into comfortable security. That kind of protection is a myth like Santa Claus and the Tooth Fairy. Here's the truth about protection:

- Protection is always *incomplete*.
- Protection is always *temporary*.
- Protection depends on *preparation*.

A bulletproof Kevlar vest provides a perfect example. According to the salesman, the vest "provides protection against bullets up to .44 magnum caliber!" For this reason, countless law officers wear these vests every day (as they certainly should), but consider these points:

- The protection afforded by the vest is *incomplete*. The vest won't stop rifle bullets or Teflon-coated bullets. President Reagan was shot with a .22 through the armhole of his vest. The bad guys can aim at your head or run you over with a car.

- The protection is *temporary*. The vest protects your chest only while you are wearing it.
- Protection requires *preparation*. When you hear the gunshot, it is too late to stop and put on the vest.

These three principles are true of all protective devices and strategies. When you acquire a device for "protection" there are always hidden pitfalls that can kill you. Here are some examples:

- *Gas masks "protect" you from poison gas.* Nerve and mustard gas can attack through your exposed skin, so the mask doesn't really help there. If you use a gas mask to enter an underground room full of carbon dioxide or sewer gas, or a smoke-filled room in a burning house, you will pass out and die. The mask doesn't supply any oxygen. If there is no oxygen in the surrounding air, the mask doesn't help. You're dead.
- *HEPA masks "protect" you from dangerous viruses.* The best particle-filtration masks, HEPA respirators, protect you from 99.97 percent of particles the size of smallpox viruses. Challenged by 100,000 airborne virus particles, the mask strains out 99,970 and lets 30 get into your lungs.
- *SCBA "protects" you from all gases and particles.* SCBA is better than any gas or filter mask because it provides safe bottled air for you to breathe. After about half an hour the air runs out, and you suddenly have to take off the mask or suffocate. The mask *leaks* if you have a beard or wear glasses, if the mask is the wrong size for you, or if you bump it against something. It is not supposed to fog up, but it often does. If you can't take it off to wipe away the moisture, you can't see. It makes it hard to drive.
- *Hazmat coveralls "protect" you from nerve gas.* Protective garments erect a barrier between your skin and some danger, such as drops of nerve gas clinging to vegetation. On a sunny day, the temperature inside the protective

suit rises to about 130°F. The suit invites heat stroke. After a couple of hours, you must take it off or pass out. Taking off a poison-contaminated suit without expert assistance is suicidal.

- *Atropine "protects" soldiers from nerve gas.* You have seen those atropine self-injection kits carried by soldiers. Atropine is an alkaloid poison derived from deadly nightshade (*Atropa belladonna*). In a gas emergency, frightened soldiers self-administer atropine injections as first aid. This makes them feel bad, so they panic and inject some more atropine. Now they feel worse, so they inject *more* atropine. During the Scud missile attacks on Tel Aviv in 1991 (which produced zero actual gas casualties), there were 230 people hospitalized because of self-inflicted atropine overdoses.[2] This was about 25 percent of the total casualties.
- *Vaccinia vaccine "protects" people from smallpox.* Without the vaccine, the smallpox death rate is 30 percent. For vaccinated victims, the death rate is still 3 percent. One out of 30 vaccinated people dies when exposed to smallpox. Immunity conferred by the vaccination lasts for years but not forever. And the live virus in the vaccine can actually attack and kill people with AIDS and similar immunodepressed conditions.[3]

So what point am I trying to make? Whenever we say that some gadget "protects" you from a threat, there is always a list of lethal exceptions you didn't know about. The gadget only encourages you to hang around in the danger zone when you should be moving away as fast as you can. *Don't put your faith in equipment.*

We will keep looking at this question as we evaluate our survival strategies to see how much protection each strategy provides a family. We expect that the protection afforded by each strategy will require significant *preparation*, will be *tem-*

porary at best, and will be regrettably *incomplete*. We must confront this situation clearly. Survival allows no room for comforting illusions.

DODGING BULLETS

Time and again I meet people whose family survival plan begins, "First we dodge the bullet; then we drive to Grandma's house." In theory, they maintain, it is easy to avoid being shot. You just step out of the path of the bullet. What could be simpler?

In the movies the bad guys shoot first and always miss. The hero spins around, draws his gun, and makes every shot count. In real life the bad guys *do* shoot first. They pick the victim. They pick the weapons. They pick the time and place. They shoot from hiding. They take careful aim and squeeze the trigger slowly. *They don't miss.* The first shot takes the victim completely by surprise, and it hits dead center. There is no opportunity to step out of the path of the bullet (even if it were possible) because you are dead before you get any warning.

If you buy gas masks or HEPA respirators or even SCBA, there is a flaw in your survival thinking. You are trying to dodge a bullet. Look again at the many chemical, biological, and radiological weapons the terrorists can use against us. If they take aim at your building or your neighborhood, they will not miss. You will be injured or exposed hours, days, or weeks before you realize that you need to put on your gas mask. As a preventive measure, the mask will do you *no good at all.*

It would not be so bad if the masks were simply useless, but they increase your risk by giving you a false sense of comfort. You don't have to find a new job or move your family out of the danger zone. After all, when the anthrax or botulism blows into your office, you can always put on your mask and leave. It is as easy as dodging a bullet.[5]

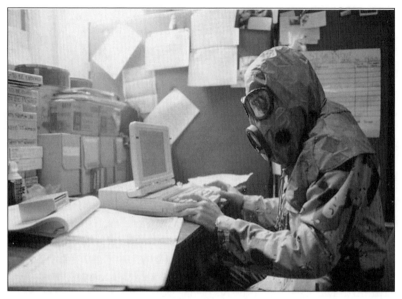

This is the only way a respirator can protect you from anthrax at work. This is not a "staged" photo. This is the XVIII Airborne Corps historian at work in M17A1 protective mask during an Iraqi SS-1B Scud attack on 20 January 1991. (Courtesy of U.S. Army Center of Military History, XVIII Airborne Corps photograph DS-F-128-19 by Pfc. John F. Freund.)[4]

AVOIDING GROUND ZERO

You cannot be perfectly safe outside of a coffin, but you can reduce your chance of being a victim. The idea is simple. The people who worked in the bottom half of the Twin Towers got out alive before the buildings collapsed. The people who worked in the top half didn't. Is it better to work in the top half of a skyscraper or the bottom half?

We can add some sophistication to our analysis by considering how much *time* you spend in various danger zones each day. Look at your map of hazardous target areas. Mark your home, work, and usual routes of travel on the map.

You'll want to mark the children's schools, too.

Do you live in a target zone? There were people living in expensive apartments across the street from the Twin Towers. Those apartments are uninhabitable now because of the damage done by the falling rubble. If you live in a conspicuous skyscraper or next to one or very near any other probable target, then you spend about two-thirds of each day at ground zero. This is very bad. If the target is attacked, there is a 66 percent chance that you'll be there at the time. That needs to change. Look for a safer place to live and, if possible, look for a place that is 20 or 30 minutes to the west of the city center. That way most of the action will happen downwind from you.

Suppose you live in a safe place but work in a target zone? You spend about one-third of your time at ground zero. That's better than living there, but it isn't really good. If the place is attacked, will you get out or will your family be posting your picture on subway walls, hoping to one day identify your remains from your DNA?

If your job places you at risk, you should find a new job. The job can be closer to the city center than your home, but don't get into a situation where you have to commute right through downtown twice a day. If you have to go home in a hurry, you'll be heading into the danger zone instead of away from it.

What about travel? Subways and tunnels are traditional terrorist targets because the nerve gas doesn't blow away quickly. How much time do you spend there? Zones you travel through are not as dangerous as zones you stop in, but maybe you can reduce your risk by changing your route.

Your personal risk is in proportion to the time you spend at the target. It is perfectly safe to visit New York as a tourist and take a ride on the subway . . . safe from terrorists, anyway. The odds are very much against an attack during the brief minutes of your visit. If you ride the subway every day, the minutes add up and so does the danger. When the terrorists attack the subway, it will be rush hour and you will probably be somewhere nearby. If you have a job in the subway, there is a very good chance you will be one of the victims of the attack. People who actually *live* in the subway tunnels, if such exist, are in the most danger of all.

You can't be "safe." There is no such thing. As far as terror is concerned, however, you can modify your life to reduce your risks. You can take your time and make every move for the better. It's not just a safer job, it's a better one with a higher salary. Start looking. It's not just a safer apartment, it's a nicer one with a better view. Shop around. The subway isn't healthy for you. Change your circumstances so you can take the train or a car or just walk. I walk to work every morning . . . about 30 feet from the bedroom to my office. Take *control* of your life. If you don't, you will be a victim every day.

PLANNING YOUR EVACUATION ROUTE

The previous section was about reducing the chance that you'll be caught in the surprise attack. Suppose, then, that some nearby area is hit and you decide to take the children out of town for a while. What route will you take?

There are general principles that apply to all planned evacuations, a theme we will return to several times in the next section. The principles are important whether the route is 2 miles long or 200 miles long. In an emergency it is important to act quickly. For that you need a *plan*.

Take a look at your map and size up the hazards and traffic patterns. You want to move to a safer area quickly, without getting caught in traffic gridlock. As a rule of thumb, going west is best; north and south are usually okay; east is least desirable. The freeways will jam up. You need to avoid bottlenecks and places where you know that rush-hour traffic tends to coagulate, even on a normal day. Finally, if it were your job to set up roadblocks to stop people from fleeing, where would you put them? Can you pick routes that will bypass those checkpoints?

It is a mistake to simply look at the map and assume that all of the targets will be hit. Establish a possible exit route and compare it with one target at a time. You may find that the route is just right for most threats, but would be fatal for one particular event. Does that disqualify the route? No, it just means you need a backup route for that situation.

Create maps showing your escape route and put them in the car. You might consider investing in a global positioning system (GPS) device to help you navigate and avoid getting lost in the excitement. Put that in the car with separate batteries. Drive the route a couple of times during rush hour to get the feel for it. Make some arrangement to be sure you will have enough gasoline to get to a safe area without running out.

The advantage you have is that terrorist attacks are generally isolated. You are safer in proportion to your distance from the scene. Twenty years ago this planning had to assume that every major city had just been blasted with a nuclear weapon, and fallout clouds were painting deadly stripes across the landscape. Planning an evacuation route for a nuclear attack was a real challenge. For a terror attack, it is more like planning for a trip on a three-day weekend.

CHAPTER 7

FAMILY
ESCAPE
STRATEGIES

The family survival movement has undergone a great deal of evolution over the years, and people new to the subject tend to follow the same well-worn path as they gain experience. The problem is remembering to keep your perspective and hold your goals firmly in mind. You need a survival strategy that will work for you . . . or that at least is the best you can manage under the circumstances. Remember that "protection" is always partial and temporary and requires preparation.

These family survival strategies were originally motivated by natural disasters and, in part, by the threat of nuclear war. As such, they take into consideration emergencies that terrorists cannot create, such as earthquakes. You are much more likely to be caught in a natural disaster than in a terrorist attack, so let's consider all the possibilities.

STRATEGY 0: DO NOTHING

One way to deal with a threat to your family is to do nothing. Just ignore it. When your number is up, it is up. Shrug your shoulders and open another beer. If something happens, you can always impose on your brother-in-law with all his silly survival supplies.

- Advantages: People like this don't have to think, worry, plan, or spend money. That leaves them plenty of time for watching network TV.
- Limitations: Their families are entirely at the mercy of outside forces.
- Disadvantages: Being irresponsible probably doesn't bother them. Being thought a coward probably isn't new. If their families die horribly, the rest of us will just bulldoze the bodies into a hole and erect a marker that says, "Examples of evolution in action."

There is a class of people who tell you, "In a nuclear war, I just hope the first bomb falls on me." They make a moral virtue of being ignorant and unprepared. In an emergency, these folks show up at your door and expect you to rescue them. I know you *say* that you will just send them packing, but it doesn't work that way in real life. You will feel differently under threat. You need to expect that and stock extra food.

When the emergency is all over and things settle down again, do me a favor and punch this guy in the nose. Thanks.

STRATEGY 1: WALK HOME

You may be caught away from home when the disaster strikes. In the Twin Towers disaster, people who escaped the damaged buildings spent many hours walking home.

Subways, trains, bridges, and tunnels were shut down, and phones were jammed, so people had to walk. You need to carry a personal survival kit sufficient to get you home from work. The classic urban survival kit is elegant: a cellular phone, an ATM card, and a pistol. In a disaster you probably won't need the pistol, but it makes you feel better about being on foot in neighborhoods you wouldn't normally visit.

This assumes that you wear sensible shoes to work. If not, you should stash some walking shoes (and socks) in your office.

- Advantages: You probably already have shoes, an ATM card, and a cellular phone. If you have the survival mindset, you probably have a pistol, too. No monetary outlay is needed.
- Limitations: If you work more than 20 miles from home, it could be a long walk.
- Disadvantages: Being on foot, alone, and unsupplied is a survival nightmare. No one suggests that this is a good situation. On the other hand, when the *Titanic* sank, a few people saved themselves by *swimming* a few yards to a lifeboat. Nobody thought that was a good survival strategy either, but it worked.

This strategy provides only minimum protection, is a temporary expedient to get you home to your family, and requires only a little preparation.

In fact, why not set down this book and go put the shoes in the car right now?

STRATEGY 2: RUN AWAY

This strategy is for the spouse at home. There is a muffled "boom" in the distance, and five minutes later a police car drives down your block. "Poison gas! Poison gas! Evacuate immediately. Go west as far as the freeway. Poison gas coming! Get out NOW."[1] You can see a green cloud coming down the street.

So you grab your keys and run out the door barefoot with two children in tow. Two hours later you are all safe at a Red Cross shelter, but you can't go home for two or three days. You forgot your credit cards. You don't have any money or ID. No blankets, no food, no jackets, no shoes. Wouldn't it have been nice if you had packed a boogie kit?

A boogie kit is a big duffle bag kept in the front closet where you can grab it on the run. The kit contains money, some food, a few soft drinks, shoes, and warm clothing. Don't forget a basic hygiene kit (toothbrush, razor, comb, etc.). If you are a little better prepared, it contains a spare ATM card or credit card and extra bottles of your essential medicines. A really good boogie kit contains your extra cellular phone.

Your boogie kit should have a set of car keys pinned to the outside of the bag in plain sight. Bitter experience shows that car keys magically disappear just when you need them the most. This is no time to be looking under the bed and tearing up sofa cushions. Make an extra set and pin it to the bag.

On the outside of the kit, in addition to the car keys, is a list of items you'd like to throw in the car if you have a few extra minutes. People call this the "teddy bear" list. Diapers, photo albums, blankets, jewelry, sanitary napkins, the pet hamster . . . it's *your* list. Think it through carefully. Assume you will be locked out of your house for three days.

A boogie kit stored in the trunk of your car is a little different because it can contain heavier items such as a case of soft drinks and bulkier items such as sleeping bags.

- Advantages: A boogie kit isn't expensive, and it greatly improves your comfort in a sudden evacuation. It lets you get on the road while everyone else is still running around their living rooms in confusion. That alone could save your life.

- Limitations: The kit is limited by weight and size. It is really a comfort kit for a Red Cross shelter or for staying at a friend's house. A full-blown family survival kit won't fit in one bag.
- Disadvantages: The boogie kit is a Band-Aid. It doesn't provide very much "protection," particularly in a very serious emergency. It is just that you feel like such an idiot if you don't have it the day you need it.

By the way, a sudden emergency like this can scatter your family, making it difficult to locate one another. You need to agree ahead of time that you will all phone the same out-of-town relative or friend or that you will all meet somewhere. You'll be absolutely frantic if you overlook this step.

Does this strategy provide only partial protection? That should be clear. Is the protection temporary? The kit is only good for two or three days. Does the strategy require preparation? Absolutely.

Set aside next Saturday for building your boogie kit. It is actually kind of fun. Terrorists don't take weekends off, and neither should you.

STRATEGY 3: DUCK AND COVER

In the 1960s I participated in grade school civil-defense drills where our teacher would suddenly shout, "Drop!" and the children would dive under their desks, pulling their chairs in after them. This was called "duck and cover." It never made very much sense to me, even in the sixth grade.

In today's context, "duck and cover" simply means to go home, lock the door, and wait for the emergency to pass. The authorities will tell you when it is safe to come out. I have been one of those authorities, and they are pretty good at rescue and evacuation issues. They have more complete information than you do, as well as expert advice from the CDC.

Your part is to be able to button up at home and stay there for some time without going outside. Let's think in terms of two to four weeks. If smallpox gets loose you'll want to stay at home for quite a while.

Staying at home is one of the easier survival strategies because your home is your survival kit. It contains all those annoying little things that you forget to take with you when you evacuate it. You just have to be certain that you will have enough food, water, warmth, and sanitation to get through the crisis.

For a terrorist attack, there is actually very little possibility that your municipal water supply will be compromised, but that won't stop the terrorists or copycats from phoning in threats. When they do, your water company will shut off the water immediately and wait for test results. That might take a few days, especially if there is any indication that someone actually *did* tamper with the water. You can hang on for a few days without food, and maybe you can bundle up against the cold, but lack of drinking water will drive you outside in short order.

- Advantages: The stay-at-home strategy is a good one for such situations as a smallpox quarantine where simple isolation will contain the problem in a few days or weeks. It is by far the most comfortable survival strategy because you are in familiar surroundings and have access to everything you own. You don't have to carry anything anywhere. You can stockpile large amounts of supplies.
- Limitations: You are somewhat at the mercy of local utilities. Water and power could be cut off.
- Disadvantages: The strategy won't work if there is persistent contamination of your neighborhood, such as

nerve gas droplets, anthrax spores, or radioactive dust. In that case you will be forced to leave and go elsewhere. If you have a big stockpile, you have to leave a lot of your supplies behind. This makes you delay the decision to cut your losses and run, which can be fatal.

Is the protection incomplete? It is good for some threats but not for others. Is it temporary? If staying at home is appropriate, you can stay a long time. That is the attraction of this strategy. Does it require preparation? You need to build a stockpile: food, water, medicine, and possibly fuel for heating and/or cooking.

What would you need to get through the first two weeks at home? Make a list and spend this weekend filling it. You can't do it all in one weekend, but if you cancel the golf game and one of the afternoon naps, you can make a good start on it.

STRATEGY 4: RELOCATE DURING THE CRISIS

I was the author of my county's official nuclear war crisis relocation plan back in the Reagan days. To prepare, I went to the official planning seminars and read all the appropriate handbooks. Crisis relocation was (and still is) the official U.S. plan for coping with nuclear attack. The federal government assumes we'll have *five days of warning*, during which everyone in the cities will pack up and go camping. The enemy will then refrain from attacking because there is no point in bombing empty cities. After a couple of weeks everyone will go home again. The enemy will continue to refrain from attacking, for reasons no one could explain to me. Isn't that nice? I thought (and still think) that this was about the dumbest plan I had ever seen.

In the context of family survival planning, "crisis relocation" means that you leave home for a couple of weeks, but you don't really have anywhere to go. You might decide to pack the car and actually take the family camping. I remember thinking that I could always go camp out in a national park if I had to. It is a lot better than waiting patiently for the next anthrax bomb to go off. The classic approach is to prepare for a long car-camping trip. You won't have any time to waste getting the car packed, so you need to prepack everything and practice getting it into the car in a hurry. Some people prepack a camper, trailer, or motor home. Some plan to convoy with friends or family.

Packing the car and driving away for a while could be a good strategy in some circumstances, but it doesn't have much to recommend it in the context of a terrorist attack. The problem is that the strategy was intended for a hurricane evacuation, earthquake, or nuclear attack, and doesn't take into account the nature of chemical and biological weapons.

The main problem with the crisis relocation survival strategy is that *you can't carry enough supplies* with you. You need to take camping gear, food, cooking fuel, and water for the whole family, plus extra gasoline for the car. I'm thinking of a family of four and an economy car. You can take the family camping for a weekend, but a smallpox quarantine could last four weeks. You can't carry four weeks of food and water in a family car. (You might manage it in a motor home, but that's like taking the duck-and-cover strategy on wheels.)

If the emergency is sudden and widespread, you should expect gridlock or traffic jams on all routes out of the city. It will be very difficult to make a clean escape from a spreading cloud of spores in stop-and-go traffic. You can beat the traffic by using motorcycles, but then you have to leave behind all your supplies. A young man with a backpack and a motorcycle could manage it but not a family with children.

You might picture yourself casting flies at your favorite trout stream while the epidemic burns out, but if infectious disease is involved you will encounter a National Guard barricade at the county line. Grim-faced soldiers will direct you to a quarantine camp in the desert or to some vacant wheat field. You'll never get to that trout stream. The whole point of a quarantine camp is to contain the spread of the infection. Once you are in the camp you will be held there until the quarantine is lifted. For plague or smallpox, it is virtually certain that somebody in the camp will have the disease. You will not be allowed to leave the camp if that happens. Let's just say you could be driving your family into a trap.

- Advantages: Evacuating with a carload of equipment and supplies is a lot better than driving away with just a boogie bag and a teddy bear. It could be an adequate solution for short-term, local emergencies that don't impose quarantine measures.
- Limitations: How many days of food and water can you carry in your car? Look at your family; look at the car. There's your limit. Of course, in a limited, local emergency you can get out of the area and resupply later.
- Disadvantages: In the wrong type of emergency, driving away in the family car could be a tactical disaster. For smallpox or plague, you could be better off locking the doors and staying home. Refugees will not be allowed to spread the disease.

  Is the protection partial? It might actually make matters worse. Is it temporary? You can't carry very much food and water, and the dislocation could last for weeks. Does it require preparation? It takes some effort to purchase and prepack the supplies.

Crisis relocation is a strategy that works in some situations but not in others. It is another strategy that emphasizes dodging the bullet as a first step. If it is all you can do, then

do it. You may have to get the children out of the danger
zone and then throw yourself on the mercy of strangers.
Historically, this strategy usually works.

On the other hand, maybe you'd like to consider a strategy that is a little less like jumping off a cliff in the dark.

STRATEGY 5: SET UP A RURAL RETREAT

At some point in your survival planning, you just have
to face the fact that the emergency might be bigger than you
can handle by packing the car. Time and again you come up
against the realization that you can't carry all the supplies
you really need. You'd have to make several trips to ferry
the supplies from your home to your survival camp out
there in the woods. That would be suicidal in a chemical,
biological, or radiological attack on your city . . . and then
realization dawns. You could shuttle the supplies out of the
city *ahead of time*. You could set up a cache of supplies outside the danger zone.

I once visited a paranoid young man who was convinced
that the FBI was out to get him. His home was perched on a
hill in the desert, with a 5-mile driveway leading down to the
highway. He thought he'd have at least a couple of minutes
warning before the white panel vans full of agents arrived at
his door. (Dodging the bullet, again.) Twenty feet outside his
back door was a buried canister containing a pair of shoes
and a pistol. It had a lanyard he could grab on the run. An
hour's walk away in the desert was a cache containing warm
clothes, a canteen of water, and a rifle. Six hours out was
another cache with a backpack, sleeping bag, food, and more
water. Two days away across the desert was a cave stocked
with supplies for three months. He could run out the back
door *literally naked* and disappear into the desert on a
moment's notice. I was very impressed by his planning. I
shipped him a complimentary copy of one of my books and

never heard from him again. (I am haunted by the thought that FedEx uses white delivery vans.)

A prestocked rural destination is called a "retreat." Twenty years ago people who stocked survival retreats were called "retreaters." Somebody decided that this sounded wimpy, and Kurt Saxon proposed the term "survivalist" instead.[2] For a while, "survivalist" meant a person who had stocked a year's supply of food, which included me, my friends, and every Mormon family in the United States. Later, however, the news media redefined "survivalist" to mean any jack-booted bigot with a gun. That just isn't me. I have not changed, but I guess I'm not a "survivalist" anymore. In this book, I use "survival family" to keep the focus where it should be . . . being responsible about protecting the kids.

So how do you set up a rural retreat?

The first impulse is to rent one of those storage lockers somewhere and fill it with food and supplies. It's nice to be able to store fuel in quantity. That's a good first step, and it doesn't cost too much, but you really need a place to live. That means a cabin or trailer or vacation house. That gets expensive. Maybe it is just a place to park the motor home and hook up. If you can afford the motor home, you can probably afford a place to park it.

For most families, it really isn't practical to own a vacation home stocked with emergency supplies. The income just isn't there. This is the point where survival families start thinking about pooling their resources with like-minded people to create a "survival group." In theory, a survival group has a lot more money, supplies, and skills than any one family can hope for. A survival group ought to be the ideal solution for creating a retreat. Unfortunately, the successes are very rare.

People who are willing to confront the challenge of survival are not followers. They are independent thinkers, soli-

tary eagles. Eagles don't flock. I once interviewed 150 survival families and collected detailed information about their
attitudes and preparations. They all wanted to join a group
but couldn't find anyone they agreed with or trusted. The
exceptions were members of extreme political or religious
groups who decided to make survival preparations *after* the
group already existed. Most of the independent families
didn't want to join a group like that.

When stocking a survival retreat, be sure to oversupply
food and water. Plan on having unexpected guests. Also, I
would advise you to rent that storage locker in addition to
buying the cabin. Put the firearms and medical supplies in
the locker. Your vacation/survival cabin will eventually be
burgled while you are out of town. (Mine was.) Picture yourself making a list of stolen equipment for the sheriff and the
insurance company. Worse yet, picture the sheriff recovering
the equipment and asking whether it is yours. This is the reason everything in your stockpile has to be *strictly legal*.

- Advantages: Establishing a cache of survival supplies outside the danger zone is a big step forward. You should do
  this even if you have to rent space to store the supplies.
- Limitations: You really need a place to live, not just a pile
  of food next to a campsite. Buying that second home is a
  tough financial hurdle.
- Disadvantages: Your cache can be stolen. In a smallpox
  or plague emergency you might be caught behind a quarantine barrier and never reach your retreat.
  Circumstances might trap you in your city home and prevent you from leaving.

The main problems here are the need to establish a second residence in the country and the fact that you still have
to dodge the bullet in the opening act. This strategy still has
a few problems, doesn't it?

Is the protection incomplete? There are scenarios where relocating to the woods doesn't work. Is it temporary? Once you reach the vacation cabin, you can stay there for weeks. That's pretty good. Does it require preparation? Buying and stocking a vacation cabin might take *years* of preparation. Financing two residences is very expensive. You might prepare all your life and never get there. For most people, the rural retreat is *not* a practical strategy.

STRATEGY 6: MOVE TO THE COUNTRY

Most people give up on retreat planning when they realize that they can't finance a second home. The vacation cabin in the country is financially unrealistic. This is what we call an imagination failure. To solve this problem, all you have to do is to sell your city home and buy a new home in the country. You get all the benefits of a survival retreat and have *only one mortgage to pay.*

Advantages of the Rural Home

Suppose you live in a small town, far from all those attractive terrorist targets in the city. How would that affect your survival planning?

- Living in a rural area removes the biggest obstacle to realistic planning. *You don't have to dodge the bullet anymore.* The surprise attacks will occur a long way over the horizon. You'll hear about it on the news before any piece of it reaches you. You have advance warning. You aren't living at ground zero.
- You don't have to worry about getting caught in the gridlock on your way out of town. You won't be stuck in traffic watching the big green cloud wafting across the rooftops. You don't have to pick the right moment to leave through the radiation.

- You get all the advantages of the duck-and-cover strategy without the hazards. You can stockpile all the food, water, and fuel you can afford, and you don't have to move it anywhere. You can have a woodstove and a few cords of firewood to keep warm in the winter. You can have a well, and you can pump an endless amount of water. You can see trees, clouds, and stars instead of streets, crowds, and cars.
- You can have the survival cabin in the woods *without* having to finance a second residence. One residence does it all. It's a financial breakthrough.

The rural home approach has overwhelming advantages. Does it have limitations? Some people just love the city and fear small towns. I don't understand these people, unless they have something to hide. In this era of cable TV and Internet shopping, you have the same access and entertainment no matter where you live. When you want to see a live show, you drive over to the city and make a weekend of it.

Most salaries in small towns are only a fraction of big-city salaries, but you can buy four bedrooms and seven acres for the price of a park bench in Silicon Valley. Things even out.

Modifications to the Rural Home

To make your rural home more survivable, you'll want to consider the following modifications:

- *Propane:* Make sure your forced-air heat and your hot water heater run from the largest propane tank the supplier will install. Mine is 500 gallons.
- *Wood stove:* Upgrade to an airtight, EPA-approved wood stove[3] and set up storage for two or more cords of wood, depending on how severe the winter is in your location. The stove keeps you warm in the winter, and you can boil water on it.

- *Water tank:* Call your well maintenance crew and ask about installing a 5,000 gallon in-line water tank uphill from your house. It makes showers run and the toilets flush without electricity.
- *Generator:* An 8-kilowatt generator with an automatic switchbox makes life in the country much more comfortable. When you lose power for a week, it's nice to be able to run the well pump and the freezers. My generator runs on propane from that 500-gallon tank.
- *Fire hose/extinguisher:* On my back deck, I have a 200-pound dry-chemical fire extinguisher with a 25-foot hose. I can knock down a house fire until the rural fire engines arrive. I also installed a gasoline-powered pump attached to the water tank, with 300 feet of 1 1/2-inch fire hose for fighting wildfires.
- *Firearm:* A rural home should have a firearm safely stored but readily available. Mine is a 12-gauge slug gun hung above the door. It makes inch-wide holes through bears, cougars, and motorcycles.

Architect Joel Skousen has made a career of designing survival homes. You should make a point of visiting his Web site to see how it is done.[4]

CHAPTER 8

PUTTING YOUR PLAN INTO ACTION

I have spent a lot of time studying and teaching karate over the years. We say that karate is a "do," a way to channel your life into productive activities and values. It looks as though you are studying how to fight, but actually you are studying how to live. A person who knows how to live doesn't have to fight.

I see the survival movement in much the same way. My interest in survival preparations gradually weaned me from the bustle of the city to the beauty of the mountains. It has improved my health and my peace of mind, and it has helped me raise strong and independent children with high moral values. But it took 20 years to go from escape strategy 1 to strategy 6.

How would you support your family out in the country? Most rural survival homes are actually owned by retired people who have taken up survival planning on behalf of their children and grandchildren. This is the best kind of survival group because the trust relationships are all in the family. The retirement income and the proceeds of that house you sold in the city make it easy to stock and equip the retreat property. That's the easy way and the most common.

For a young couple to deliberately move from the city or suburbs to rural America takes a strategy and some courage. My wife and I moved to the mountains when we were about 30 years old. She took office jobs, and I wrote books and magazine articles. Later I had to go back to the city for a couple of years to make ends meet, but I left the family safely in the woods. Then I became a telecommuter, writing software and computer documentation from my home in the forest. I developed enough good friends in the industry to become a true consultant. These days, people fly me around the country to work on their projects. I charge Silicon Valley rates while living in God's Country. It can be done. The key to success is to get up off your butt and *try*.

A quick look around reveals that there are quite a few jobs that go begging out here in the countryside. There are never enough doctors. Every town needs a dentist, an optometrist, and a veterinarian. Nurses are in very short supply. Pharmacists seem to have their pick of jobs. (Lawyers are in demand too, but they only make $150 an hour.) Tax accountants seem as frantic here as they do everywhere else. The school district is increasingly desperate for teachers. The construction industry is booming because of the low interest rates caused by the current slump in the economy. You never seem to be able to get a plumber when you need one. My favorite automobile mechanic has more business than his ulcer can handle. There are road-building crews everywhere and trucking delivery jobs. I have a friend down the road who sits in his home editing electronic manuscripts for publishing houses. My next-door neighbor has a thriving business doing wedding photography. Opportunities exist. You just have to find them or make them.

If you want to move to the country, my suggestion is to go exploring on weekends. Get a phone book for each candidate community and scroll through the businesses. Buy local newspapers. Call people up and ask them for advice. Tell them that their town is beautiful and that you'd really like to live there. Do they know of any jobs? Can they recommend someone who would know? When you introduce yourself to the second party, mention the first party's name. It gets you a hearing. Build a chain of referrals by getting each person you interview to recommend another person you can contact.

If there are jobs, apply for them. A good match doesn't matter. Sooner or later you will connect. Once you get out here, you can impress your employer, build your circle of friends, and find better opportunities. You gradually become a part of the community and put down roots. You buy a bigger house than you could in the city. Going back becomes unthinkable. You're *home* now.

Years later, you realize that you haven't worried much about terrorists or disasters in a long time. The fear goes away. It is a goal worth fighting for.

Does it still seem insurmountable? OK, stay in the city for a few years but make a plan. Make some adjustments to reduce your risk. Moving out of the target zone may take 10 years, but you can do it. You're a secretary, but you can take nursing or accounting classes at night and on weekends. It will take a few years, but with your new degree you have new opportunities. If you are not the college type, get a job with the U.S. Postal Service. Slave away at the downtown office for seven or eight years. Get enough seniority to bid for positions in the country. Get one and move. It *can* be done. It just takes courage and commitment. If the kids are little now, you can make the move before they get involved with gangs and drugs in junior high. That's a worthy goal, too.

There are plenty of places where skies are still blue, air is still clean, schools are still safe, and people wave at you and call you by name. Make the effort. Then you can watch the nightly news without dreading what you might hear.

EPILOG

THE FUTURE OF TERROR

A long time ago, I wrote a list called "10 Upcoming Disasters" for *The Book of Lists*, a People's Almanac publication. It took the company over a year to get the book published, and the list wasn't in it. When I asked about its omission, an editor noted that some of the predicted disasters had already happened, so the list was old news by then. (My best prediction was the Mt. St. Helens eruption.)[1]

Can we predict where the terrorism trend will take us? Future trends are not difficult to predict: what has happened before will happen again. When you see how the dominoes are set up, you can see where they will fall.

In the United States, our dance with terrorism has only begun. Everything points to a decade of increasing violence as multiple groups become more adept at launching terrorist attacks on U.S. soil. What kinds of developments might we expect over the next few years?

People are looking for the danger in the wrong place. The danger is real, but it is not in the Middle East. It is here.

FUTURE OF INTERNATIONAL TERRORISM

At the time of this writing, the United States is mopping up in Afghanistan, trying to dislodge the Taliban permanently. This effort is bound to damage al Qaeda financially, although it will only strengthen the members' resolve. Trying to destroy a terror network with bombs is like trying to kill an ant colony by firing a pistol at individual ants. The best we can hope for is to cut al Qaeda off from the lucrative opium trade. We might get very lucky and blow up some terror celebrities, but that will just make room for new leaders. It won't make any real difference.

The militant Islamists have very visible political goals, involving the overthrow of Middle Eastern governments they deem not "Islamic" enough. There is also a utopian dream of uniting the independent Islamic states into one empire, but the cultures are too deeply divided to make that easy. They have fought one another for a thousand years, and they enjoy it.[2]

Our retaliation against international terror plays into their hands because it forces various governments to take a stand relative to the United States.[3] This makes it easy to target specific governments as being "anti-Islamic" and allied with the Great Satan. The angry rabble is a real danger to the governments of Pakistan and Saudi Arabia, and further developments may be expected in other nearby countries.[4] Changes in government alignment can and will destabilize the Middle East and pose a threat to the Persian Gulf and the Indian Subcontinent.

These local wars and revolutions will not hurt Americans too badly until something happens that allows Iran to take control of Iraq. Then we will see very large mechanized armies rolling into Saudi Arabia and across Syria toward Israel. World War III will begin in earnest. This is the reason the United States has been so careful not to destabilize Iraq. Even hopelessly doomed resistance movements persist and commit violence without end, sometimes for hundreds of years. Regardless of other developments, Middle Eastern terrorists will continue to operate against the citizens of the United States as long as Israel exists because they see themselves as resisting a Crusader invasion. This violence will not stop in our lifetimes.

There is one piece of good news you may not have considered. Try to picture the U.S. coastline being bombarded by the Arab navy. That thought ought to elicit a smile.

FUTURE OF HOMELAND SECURITY

The militant Islamists have no interest in overthrowing the government of the United States; their ambitions are closer to home. That doesn't mean that their attacks will not score heavily against our way of life. We can already see this beginning to happen.

In response to the 9/11 attacks, our government suddenly has a whole new bureaucracy, the Office of Homeland Security.[5] The creation of this new agency may have sounded like a good idea at the time, but *internal security* is a branch of government power that the United States has never needed in its 200-year history. And every totalitarian nation has relied on a just such department with a similar mission. The office that protected the state from internal attack, largely by using informers and internal passports, was called the Committee for State Security (the KGB) in the Soviet Union, the Secret State Police (Gestapo) under Nazi Germany, and the State Security Ministry (Stasi) under communist East Germany. It is an institution we now share with such countries as Chile, Iran, Iraq, Romania, and South Africa. At the time of this writing, there is talk in the United States of creating an internal passport in the form of a national identity card.

Will the Office of Homeland Security turn into a state terror organization? Not right away, but its employees will put tools in place that can be perverted to that end. The United States is making an extremely serious turn here—and not for the better. Why not? Because although security crackdowns destroy liberty, they never really produce increased security.[6] Instead, they intensify the threat.

I have consulted in computer security, so I know what a "smart card" is and what it can do. The smart card is a very secure means of identification, but it has shocking flaws. A smart card is like a key that only one person in the world can use. The idea is to issue these one-person keys to every U.S. citizen and then use them for access to aircraft and other sensitive resources. Basically, you issue a smart ID to every law-abiding citizen, so that anyone without an ID must be a bad guy.

So, there you are, a solid, upstanding citizen with a smart ID card. You are a trusted airport employee. You have never done anything illegal, and you don't like terrorists. So one day you go to work and, using your impeccable ID, slip an unauthorized package into the cargo hold of a plane. It's a bomb, and when it explodes it kills all the people on board the plane. Why did you do it? You did it because your wife and two little daughters disappeared over the weekend, and someone mailed you a plastic bag with three severed fingers in it. "Do what we say or we'll send you their eyes tomorrow." One-person keys are great for computer security, but they don't stop organized killers. They just point a gun at the victim's head, and he opens the lock for them. Where's the security in that?

There's another problem with smart-card IDs. You have

to carefully validate the identification of each person who receives a card or the whole system is worthless. At present, the FBI is about a year behind in doing security clearance investigations for government agencies and contractors. Who will do the investigating before issuing 200 million ID cards? How much investigation will go into each new ID? We will need *thousands* of trained card authorizers for this task, and about one in a hundred will turn out to be dishonest. Organized crime will find these dishonest people, and it will soon be possible to buy legitimate IDs under false names. It always happens. Once the black market starts to operate, the card will be no inconvenience to terrorists at all.

But you'll still have to produce the card to get on a plane.

FUTURE OF DOMESTIC TERROR

The danger of the war against Islamic terror does not lie in the Middle East. The danger lies in the U.S. Midwest.

The militia groups have always been present throughout our history, but they have been growing lately in reaction to the terrible events at Ruby Ridge and Waco, among others.[7] The FBI has acquired a new, Gestapo-like reputation for violence. The Treasury Department's BATF has had that reputation among gun owners for many years. When Americans worry that law enforcement has too much power and too little oversight, they usually write their congressmen. If they don't have much faith in Congress, they seek comfort from like-minded people. That's why the militias are growing.

It doesn't matter whether or not the Office of Homeland Security is necessary to combat terrorism. It doesn't matter whether its intentions are pure. It doesn't matter how carefully it preserves and protects the Constitution. Anything it does will inflame the militias.[8] Anything will be taken as a sign that it is time to take action. The militias have a noble cause, and now the Office of Homeland Security joins the

FBI and the BATF in providing them with a clear and present enemy. Militias members will become inflamed—their leaders will see to it.

Most militia members protest loudly, march angrily, and train sporadically but stop short of breaking the law. The militia movement will draw more support, and eventually militia rallies and conferences will distill the really rabid members into splinter groups. These splinter groups will launch attacks on targets associated with federal law enforcement agencies.

Once the terror cycle starts, it is hard to stop. In five years our entire country could look like Northern Ireland or Israel, under siege by terrorists who are sheltered and supported by a significant portion of the population. That's a horrible prediction, and I take no pleasure in it. There is a ray of hope, however: the United States might be the only place on earth that can derail the terror cycle.

FUTURE OF LIBERTY

Of all nations, the United States of America is one of the few where democracy really works. We don't have coups and revolutions because we cleverly use the ballot box to "throw the rascals out" every few years. Our Constitution gives us checks and balances designed to frustrate a tyrant. The Gestapo never had to deal with the U.S. Supreme Court. The KGB never had its secrets leaked by talkative members of Congress. The Stasi and other secret police forces never had to deal with a free press or a president hungry for reelection.

And last, but not least, no secret police force in history had to deal with an armed citizenry. This factor is completely unique to the United States. The citizens have more guns than the government has. Let's be sure we keep it that way.

I think we have some bad times ahead, but the terrorists

will suffer more than we do. America will prevail, within and without. We will defeat our bitter enemies. We will rise above our internal factions, solve our economic problems, and unite as a nation to overcome this threat. The Chinese say, "What doesn't kill us makes us stronger." Terrorists may be able to kill American citizens, but they cannot kill America. In 10 years, the challenge of terrorism will make this nation the strongest the world has ever known.

NOTES

I spent 1973 to 1978 researching *Life After Doomsday*, my guide to surviving a nuclear war. I haunted moldy libraries for years to get the information together. Today, you can find just about any information—in *seconds*—on the World Wide Web. This poses two problems for the writer/researcher:

- First, how reliable is the information? I have based this book on Web publications of large and respected institutions such as the U.S. Army Medical Corps, the Centers for Disease Control and Prevention, the U.S. Congress, the U.S. Department of State, The Johns Hopkins University, and the FBI. I also used the archives of major news services. Web sites with less lofty provenance are duly noted.
- Second, information on the Web is volatile and often

poorly identified. Articles may disappear, and URLs may change without notice. I have tried to provide enough information that you can index to similar material if an article becomes unavailable. There is no lack of material out there.

PREFACE

1. Bruce D. Clayton, *Life After Doomsday, A Survivalist Guide to Nuclear War and Other Major Disasters,* (Boulder, Colo.: Paladin Press, 1980). It is available through Paladin Press. The references are quite dated, but the effects of nuclear weapons have a timeless quality.

CHAPTER 1: AMERICA AT WAR

1. "U.S. takes 4 embassy bombing suspects to trial," CNN.com Law Center, < http://www11.cnn.com/LAW/trials.and.cases/case.files /0012/embassy.bombing/overview.html >.

2. Search the Web for "Ramzi Yousef Bojinka" to find such articles as "Plot to use planes in U.S. attacks uncovered in RP," September 12, 2001, by Raymond C. Burgos, Alcuin Papa, and Dave Veridiano, *Inquirer News Service,* > http://www.inq7.net/nat/2001/sep/13/nat_4-1.htm >.

3. Phil Hirschkorn, "Prosecution uses bin Laden interview in embassy bombings trial," CNN.com, February 21, 2001, < http://www5.cnn.com/2001/LAW/02/21/embassy. bombing/ >.

4. U.S. Department of State, *Patterns of Global Terrorism 1999,* published April 2000; Appendix C, < http://www.state.gov/www/global/terrorism/1999 report/373317.jpg >.

CHAPTER 2: THEORY OF TERRORISM

1. Make a point of reading *A Quick and Dirty Guide to War: Briefings on Present and Potential Wars* by James F. Dunnigan and Austin Bay (New York: William Morrow, 1991), either the original or the revised edition. It contains all the information that high school history classes should but don't. Get it used through Amazon.com.

2. Jonathan Swift satirized this phenomenon in *Gulliver's Travels* (published anonymously in 1726), where two kingdoms fought a bitter war about how to open a soft-boiled egg.

3. They study the Koran, of course. "Religion Rules Afghan, Pakistani School Day," *Education Week* (October 10, 2001), < http://www.edweek.org/ew/ newstory.cfm?slug = 06international.h21 >.

4. Paul Sperry, "Airport-security firm at mercy of Muslims: EEOC case forced company to rehire Arabs, instate Islamic-sensitivity training program," WorldNetDaily.com. < http://www.worldnetdaily.com/ news/article.asp? ARTICLE_ID = 25259 >.

5. Here are two instances. Six months after the 9/11 attacks, the U.S. Immigration and Naturalization Service sent out renewed student visas for two of the terrorists who were killed in the planes that slammed into the World Trade Center towers (< http://www.cnn.com/ 2002/US/03/15/ins. shakeup/index.html >). Also Gen. Joe Foss, 86, was detained at the Phoenix airport for an hour while airport security personnel tried to confiscate his Congressional Medal of Honor because it had "pointy edges and a nasty-looking pin on the back" (< http://www.cnn.com/2002/US/02/27/war.hero.cnna/ index.html >).

6. A more extensive classification of terrorist types may

be found in "Threat of Terrorism in the United States," Statement before Congress by Louis Freeh, former director of the FBI (May 10, 2001). http://www.fbi.gov/congress/congress01/freeh051001.htm>.

7. *Court TV Online,* "Kaczynski psychological report details descent into schizophrenia," (September 15, 1999), < http://www.courttv.com/trials/unabomber/>.

8. There is testimony that al Qaeda simply buys anthrax and other cultures from Eastern European labs. Niles Lathem, "Osama Bought a Batch for 10G," NYPOST.com, < http://www.nypost.com/news/worldnews/32458.htm>.

9. Tom Clancy, *Rainbow Six* (1998), available practically everywhere. In this offering, Mr. Clark saves the world from ecoterror.

10. Jonathan B. Tucker, "Historical Trends Related to Bioterrorism: An Empirical Analysis," *Emerging Infectious Diseases,* v. 5, no. 4, (July–August 1999), Centers for Disease Control and Prevention, < http://www.cdc.gov/ncidod/EID/vol5no4/tucker.htm >.

11. The idea of a blind acupuncturist is worth some thought. It conjures up images of kids playing pin the tail on the donkey.

12. Everything you want to know about the history of Ireland and then some can be found at < http://www.irelandstory.com/>.

13. "Roots of Common Law" contains a lengthy interview with Daniel Levitas on the history of the militant American groups on the extreme right. < http://www.splcenter.org/cgi-bin/goframe.pl?dirname=/.&pagename=sitemap.html >.

14. *Militia Research Page,* a private Web site containing many links to militia-related topics, hosted on the Web server of the University of Texas at Austin, < http://uts.cc.utexas.edu/~thetruth/militia/militia.html >.

15. "81-day Freemen standoff ends without bloodshed," *The Minnesota Daily* Online, June 14, 1996, < http://www.daily.umn.edu/daily/1996/06/14/world_nation/wn614b.ap/ >.
16. For a lesson on the only French resistance organization never penetrated by the Gestapo, see *Noah's Ark: The Secret Underground* by Marie-Madeleine Fourcade (out of print, but available through Amazon.com).
17. U.S. Department of State, *Patterns of Global Terrorism 2000* (April 2001), < http://www.usis.usemb.se/terror/rpt2000/overview-state.html >.
18. Federation of American Scientists, *Countering the Changing Threat of International Terrorism*, Report of the National Commission on Terrorism (published June 2000). < http://www.fas.org/irp/threat/commission.html >.
18. For a vivid, first-hand account of interviewing Osama bin Laden at a camp in Afghanistan, see "Greetings, America. My name is Osama bin Laden," by John Miller, PBS Online, WGBH/Frontline, < http://www.pbs.org/wgbh/pages/frontline/shows/binladen/who/miller.html >.
20. For a first-hand account of life inside al Qaeda, see "Embassy Bombing Trial Hears of Confession by Accused Terrorist," by Judy Aita, U.S. Department of State, *Washington File* (March 7, 2001), < http://usinfo.state.gov/topical/pol/terror/01030861.htm >.
21. Identification based on the photos in *The Week*'s cover story on the War Against Terrorism (October 7, 2001), < http://www.the-week.com/21oct07/cover.htm#4 >.
22. "Al Qaida's bio-warfare facility hit," *Hindustan Times* (October 11, 2001), < http://www.hindustantimes.com/nonfram/111001/ dlame51.asp >.

23. "Responsibility for the Terrorist Atrocities in the United States, 11 September 2001," from the official Web site of the prime minister of Great Britain, < http://www.number-10.gov.uk/news.asp? NewsId = 2686&SectionId = 30 >.

24. Atef was killed in November 2001 by a U.S. airstrike in Afghanistan. At the time of publication of this book, Osama bin Laden and his other lieutenants have simply disappeared.

CHAPTER 3: WEAPONS OF TERROR

1. Apparently it is not a very good model. Most sources indicate that a Russian "suitcase" bomb is the size of a steamer trunk.

2. U.S. Department of Transportation, *2000 Emergency Response Guidebook*, < http://hazmat.dot.gov/ gydebook.htm >.

3. The most valuable reference I found on chemical and biological weapons is the *Textbook of Military Medicine, Medical Aspects of Chemical and Biological Warfare*, 1996, Office of the Surgeon General, Department of the Army, posted on the Medical NBC Information Server. An HTML version is available at < http://ccc.apgea.army.mil/Documents/HTML_ Restricted/index_2.htm > and a PDF version is available at < http://www.nbc-med.org/SiteContent/ HomePage/WhatsNew/MedAspects/contents.html >. In the following notes I have abbreviated this work as TMM-MACB. See Chapter 5, "Nerve Agents."

4. The antidote syringe is a very simple device. It injects automatically when you push the needle into your thigh. The step-by-step instructions on how to perform this simple injection are *12 pages* long. By the time you read them, you're dead. < http://www.nbc- med.org/SiteContent/MedRef/OnlineRef/FieldManuals/ fm8_285/appende.htm >.

5. TMM-MACB, Chapter 7, "Vesicants."
6. *Chlorine Chemical Backgrounder,* National Safety Council, Crossroads Web site, < http://www.cross-roads.nsc.org/ChemicalTemplate.cfm?id = 91&chempath = chemicals >.
7. TMM-MACB, Chapter 9, "Toxic Inhalational Injury."
8. TMM-MACB, Chapter 10, "Cyanide Poisoning."
9. The following Web site contains graphic color photos of Kurdish villagers cut down by Iraqi cyanide bombs in 1988: < http://www.kdp.pp.se/chemical.html >. The children must have died in midstride. It is not for the faint of heart.
10. TMM-MACB, Chapter 11, "Incapacitating Agents."
11. MKULTRA actually took place, but it is difficult to find information about it because of its deep classification, the destruction of CIA records, and the resulting anti-CIA hysteria. See *Secrecy and Accountability in U.S. Intelligence* by Steven Aftergood, at the Federation of American Scientists Web site, < http://www.fas.org/sgp/cipsecr.html >.
12. "Cholinergic Transmission," on the Web site of Roger P. Smith, Ph.D., at Dartmouth University, < http://www.dartmouth.edu/ ~ rpsmith/Cholinergic_Transmission.html >.
13. TMM-MACB, Chapter 18, "Historical Overview of Biological Warfare," page 421 for the list of Iraqi biological munitions at the start of the Gulf War.
14. Office of Technology Assessment, "Technologies Underlying Weapons of Mass Destruction" (Chapter 3), *Technical Aspects of Biological Weapon Proliferation* (p. 96), on a Princeton University Web server, < http://www.wws.princeton.edu/ ~ ota/disk1/1993/9344_n.html >. Some things should not be public. This document is one of them.
15. After an hour of research on the Web, I am pretty sure

I could produce a small batch of aerosol-size particles using inexpensive equipment available in hobby shops. I don't think it serves any good purpose to explain how.

16. Health Canada Health Protection Branch Laboratory Centre for Disease Control, "Classification of Biological Agents According to Risk" (Chapter 4), *Laboratory Biosafety Guidelines* (1996), < http://www. hc-sc.gc.ca/hpb/lcdc/biosafty/docs/lbg4_e.html >.

17. Health Canada Health Protection Branch Laboratory Centre for Disease Control, "Physical Containment Levels" (Chapter 5), *Laboratory Biosafety Guidelines* (1996), < http://www.hc-sc.gc.ca/hpb/lcdc/biosafty/docs/lbg5_e.html >.

18. *FBI Advisory* contains images of suspicious packages, CNN.com, < http://www.cnn.com/2001/HEALTH/ conditions/10/16/fbi.advice/ >.

19. "Investigators look for links between anthrax and terrorism," CNN.com (October 16, 2001). Contains a photo of two actual anthrax letters. < http://www.cnn. com/2001/HEALTH/conditions/10/16/anthrax/index. html >.

20. Center for Civilian Biodefense Studies, Johns Hopkins University, *Anthrax*. < http://www.hopkins-biodefense.org/pages/agents/agentanthrax.html >.

21. Centers for Disease Control and Prevention, *Anthrax, Frequently Asked Questions* (October 18, 2001), < http://www.cdc.gov/ncidod/dbmd/diseaseinfo/anthrax _g.htm >.

22. Health Canada Office of Laboratory Security, *Bacillus anthracis*, Material Safety Data Sheet, < http://www. hc-sc.gc.ca/pphb-dgspsp/msds-ftss/msds12e.html >.

23. TMM-MACB, Chapter 22, "Anthrax."

24. Although there soon may be one. "Fast Army scanner detects chemical and biological agents in minutes,"

CNN.com (October 28, 2001), < http://www.cnn.com/
2001/US/10/28/ret.attacks.biochem.ap/index.html >.

25. Personal communication from my county health
officer.

26. TMM-MACB, Chapter 20, "Use of Biological
Weapons," p. 444, Table 20-1, which cites *Health
Aspects of Chemical and Biological Weapons*. Geneva,
Switzerland: World Health Organization (1970: 98).
Many documents cite this one study, but it isn't easy
to find.

27. Center for Disease Control and Prevention, *National
Pharmaceutical Stockpile (NPS) Program*,
< http://www.cdc.gov/nceh/nps/synopses.htm#Determi
ning%20And%20Maintaining%20NPS%20Assets >.

28. Subcommittee on National Security, Veterans Affairs,
and International Relations, U.S. Congress, "Briefing
memorandum for the hearing 'Combating Terrorism:
Management of Medical Supplies,' scheduled for
Tuesday, May 1, 2001," < http://www.house.gov/
reform/ns/web_resources/briefing_memo_may_1_2001
.htm >.

29. Milton Leitenberg, "An Assessment of the Biological
Weapons Threat to the United States," Testimony
before the Committee on Government Reform U.S.
House of Representatives (October 12, 1999), on the
Web site of the Federation of American Scientists.
< http://www.fas.org/bwc/papers/oct12tes.htm >.

30. There is testimony that al Qaeda simply buys anthrax
and other cultures from Eastern European labs. Niles
Lathem, "Osama Bought a Batch for 10G,"
NYPOST.com, < http://www.nypost.com/news/
worldnews/32458.htm >.

31. Center for Civilian Biodefense Studies, Johns Hopkins
University, *Tularemia*, < http://www.hopkins-
biodefense.org/pages/agents/agenttularemia.html >.

32. TMM-MACB, Chapter 24, "Tularemia."
33. Center for Civilian Biodefense Studies, Johns Hopkins University, *Plague*, < http://www.hopkins-biodefense.org/pages/agents/agentplague.html >.
34. Health Canada Office of Laboratory Security, *Yersinia pestis*, Material Safety Data Sheet, < http://www.hc-sc.gc.ca/pphb-dgspsp/msds-ftss/msds169e.html >.
35. TMM-MACB, Chapter 23, "Plague."
36. "Plague as a Biological Weapon," *Journal of the American Medical Association*, Vol. 283 No. 17 (May 3, 2000), < http://jama.ama-assn.org/issues/v283n17/ffull/jst90013.html >.
37. TMM-MACB, Chapter 23, "Plague" (cited above), page 482.
38. David E. Kaplan, Senior Editor, "Interview with Larry Wayne Harris," *U.S. News & World Report* (September 2, 1997), < http://www.usnews.com/usnews/news/chemhar.htm >.
39. "Statement of Dr. Kenneth Alibek" to subcommittees of the U.S. Congress (October 20, 1999), < http://www.house.gov/hasc/testimony/106thcongress/99-10-20alibek.htm >.
40. Center for Civilian Biodefense Studies, Johns Hopkins University, *Smallpox*, < http://www.hopkins-biodefense.org/pages/agents/agentsmallpox.html >.
41. TMM-MACB, Chapter 27, "Smallpox."
42. "Former Soviet republic agrees to clean up stockpiles of anthrax, biochemical weapons," Associated Press (10/23/2001), < http://www.boston.com/dailynews/296/wash/Former_Soviet_republic_agrees_:.shtml >.
43. The "era of vaccination" began earlier than you think. The Chinese have been performing "variolation" for about 1,000 years. The safer method using cowpox was in wide use in Europe from 1800 onward.
44. "Poxviruses," class notes of BS335 Virology, University

NOTES

of Leicester, with a nice picture of Ramses V.,
< http://www-
micro.msb.le.ac.uk/335/Poxviruses.html >.
45. TMM-MACB, Chapter 27, "Smallpox," p. 550.
46. Health Canada Office of Laboratory Security, *Ebola virus*, Material Safety Data Sheet, < http://www.
hc-sc.gc.ca/pphb-dgspsp/msds-ftss/msds53e.html >.
47. TMM-MACB, Chapter 29, "Viral Hemorrhagic Fevers."
48. Centers for Disease Control and Prevention, *Infection Control for Viral Haemorrhagic Fevers in the African Health Care Setting*, < http://www.cdc.gov/
ncidod/dvrd/spb/mnpages/vhfmanual.htm >.
49. Centers for Disease Control and Prevention, *Fact Sheet, Ebola Hemorrhagic Fever*, < http://www.cdc.gov/
ncidod/dvrd/spb/mnpages/dispages/ebola.htm >.
50. Tim Butcher, "Ebola-style killer virus sweeps Afghan border," *Telegraph* on-line (April 10, 2001),
< http://www.portal.telegraph.co.uk/news/main.jhtml?x
ml =/news/2001/10/04/wref04.xml&sSheet =/news/2001
/10/04/ixhome.html >.
51. Jeff Rense, "Former Chief of Soviet BioWar Production Issues Warning," a colorful interview with Dr. Kenneth Alibek on Rense's Web site, < http://www.rense.com/
political/weapons/formerchief.htm >.
52. The table is based on *Ebola Hemorrhagic Fever, Table Showing Known Cases and Outbreaks, in Chronological Order*, Centers for Disease Control and Prevention.
< http://www.cdc.gov/ncidod/dvrd/spb/mnpages/
dispages/ebotabl.htm >.
53. TMM-MACB, Chapter 30, "Defense Against Toxin Weapons."
54. Center for Civilian Biodefense Studies, Johns Hopkins University, *Botulinum toxin*, < http://www.hopkins-
biodefense.org/pages/agents/agentbotox.html >.
55. TMM-MACB, Chapter 33, "Botulinum Toxins."

167

56. TMM-MACB, Chapter 32, "Ricin Toxin."
57. Carey Sublette, "Osama, Suitcase Bombs, and Ex-Soviet Loose Nukes," on the Web site of the Federation of American Scientists, < http://www.fas.org/nuke/hew/News/Lebedbomb.html >.
58. It is chilling to read the official transcript of al Fadl's testimony at the trial. Search down for the word "uranium" and start reading: < http://cryptome.org/usa-v-ubl-03.htm >.
59. "Witness says he warned U.S. two years before embassy attacks," CNN.com (February 7, 2001), < http://www.cnn.com/2001/LAW/02/07/embassy. bombing.03/ >.
60. Containers of uranium were reported found in an underground bunker near Kandahar by U.S. forces in Decemer 2001. U.S. officials later called this report a hoax because the uranium canisters were empty. Why don't I feel better? "Uranium and cyanide found in drums at bin Laden base," by Barbie Dutter and Ben Fenton, 12/24/2001, < http://www.portal.telegraph.co. uk/ >. "Pentagon says WMDs not likely in Afghanistan," CNN.com, 1/18/2002, < http://asia.cnn.com/2002/WORLD/asiapcf/cen-tral/01/17/ret.afghan.wmd/ >.
61. I created this scenario using the weapon-effects calculator included in Samuel Glasstone and Philip J. Dolan, eds., *The Effects of Nuclear Weapons*, U.S. Department of Defense and the Energy Research and Development Administration (Washington, D.C.: U.S. Government Printing Office, 1977). This is the bible of nuclear weapons effects. Parts of the book are on line courtesy of the Federation of American Scientists: < http://www.fas.org/nuke/trinity/nukeffct/enw77. htm >.
62. For an interesting comparison with this scenario, see

similar illustrations created by Roger Avedon for his dissertation on nuclear terrorism at < http://www. slip.net/ ~ debk/roger/nuc-example.html >.

63. Bruce Clayton, *Fallout Survival* (Boulder, Colo.: Paladin Press, 1984). Out of print, but you can find used copies on the Internet for very high prices. (See note 1 under the Preface for information about *Life After Doomsday*.)

64. There is a Web site that lets you calculate the number of people living within a certain radius of a specific post office. It reports that the population density in central Manhattan around ZIP code 10018 is about 40,000 people per square mile. Try it yourself: < http://zipfind.net >.

65. Col. David G. Jarrett, Medical Corps, United States Army, "Medical Management of Radiological Casualties Handbook" (December 1999), < http://www.afrri.usuhs.mil/ >.

66. "The NRC did not specifically contemplate attacks by aircraft such as Boeing 757s or 767s and nuclear power plants were not designed to withstand such crashes. Detailed engineering analyses of a large airliner crash have not yet been performed." "NRC Reacts to Terrorist Attacks," press release No. 01-112 of the U.S. Nuclear Regulatory Commission (September 21, 2001), < http://www.nrc.gov/docs/news/archive/01-112.html >.

67. What does "contaminate" mean? The antinuclear power lobby floods the Web with breathless diatribes about Chernobyl, while the pronuclear sites minimize it beyond reason. Detectable contamination was worldwide. People are having a high incidence of thyroid cancer over large areas of Belarus, the Russian Federation, and the Ukraine. The Soviets permanently abandoned the region within 30 kilometers (19 miles) of the reactor, eventually relocating about 300,000 peo-

ple to new homes outside the radiation zone. You'll find a serious technical discussion at < http://www.unscear.org/pdffiles/annexj.pdf >. The site has detailed maps that take a long time to download but are worth it.

68. When I was a student pilot, my instructor once joked, "IFR means *I follow roads*." We did, too.

CHAPTER 4: TERROR TAKES AIM

1. National Task Force on Violence Against Health Care Providers, "Report on Federal Efforts to Prevent and Prosecute Clinic Violence 1998–2000," U.S. Department of Justice Web site, < http://www.usdoj.gov/crt/crim/tfreppub.htm >.

2. In Decemer 2001 U.S. forces discovered a home video of Osama bin Laden discussing the 9/11 attacks with admirers. Bin Laden described planning the attack and said he was surprised that the buildings collapsed. He had expected to destroy only a few floors of each building. Transcripts of this interview are widely available on the Web.

3. Everything you want to know about U.S. aircraft carriers, < http://www.chinfo.navy.mil/navpalib/ factfile/ships/ship-cv.html >.

4. "Bin Laden's Invisible Network," *Newsweek* International (October 29, 2000). < http://www.msnbc.com/news/645596.asp >.

5. Mark Davis, "Propaganda war may miss targets" (October 21, 2001), CNN.com, < http://www.cnn.com/ 2001/US/10/21/ret.propaganda.war/index.html >.

6. "World's Tallest Buildings," an article at the Infoplease.com Web site, < http://www.infoplease.com/ipa/A0001338.html >.

CHAPTER 5: SURVIVAL BASICS

1. To locate survival books and supplies, go to an Internet search engine (such as www.google.com) and search for "Life After Doomsday by Bruce Clayton." Any Web site that sells my book will have many similar offerings of interest to you.

2. Ron's Web site is < http://www.survival.com/aboutus.htm >.

3. Cresson Kearny, *Nuclear War Survival Skills* (U.S. Government Printing Office: 1987). This book is the result of Kearny's years of research at Oak Ridge National Laboratory. It was published obscurely by the U.S. Government Printing Office and is now available from other sources through Amazon.com. You can download it from < http://www.oism.org/ddp/ >.

4. How? I'd go straight to Recreational Equipment, Inc. (REI). Look at the "base camp" water purification units first at < http://www.rei-camping.com/water_purification.htm >.

5. *How to Be Your Own Doctor (Sometimes)* by Keith W. Sehnert is excellent but out of print. Look for used copies at Amazon.com. Sehnert designed an augmented home medical kit that your doctor will agree with.

6. "Families can file death certificates for missing," CNN.com (September 25, 2001) includes a statement about the crime rate, < http://www.cnn.com/2001/US/09/25/vic.death.documents/index.html >.

7. These rules are as follows: (1) All guns are always loaded. (2) Never let the muzzle cover anything you are not willing to destroy. (3) Keep your finger off the trigger until your sights are on the target. (4) Be sure of your target. They were provided by Greg Morrison, *API 250 General Pistol Course, Student Notebook*, The American Pistol Institute (now the Gunsite Academy), 1988.

CHAPTER 6: REDUCING YOUR RISK

1. This information is freely available on the Internet. See the Web site of the National Law Enforcement and Corrections Technology Center (NLECTC), < http:// www.ojp.usdoj.gov/nij/new.htm#firstresponder >.
2. TMM-MACB, Chapter 1, "Overview: Defense Against the Effects of Chemical and Biological Warfare Agents."
3. Health Canada Office of Laboratory Security, *Vaccinia virus*, Material Safety Data Sheet, < http://www. hc-sc.gc.ca/pphb-dgspsp/msds-ftss/msds160e.html >.
4. XVIII Airborne Corps History Office Photographs, Gulf War Photo Sampler, < http://www.army.mil/ cmh-pg/photos/gulf_war/ods.htm >.
5. Here is one of many examples of bullet dodging: a training scenario where the bad guys give us *48 hours warning* before releasing the anthrax. "A Biological Weapons Threat in San Francisco, California," by Kenneth M. Berry, M.D., President, American Academy of Emergency Physicians, FEMA/PNNL Workshop (Richland, Wash., September 24, 1997). < http://www.home.eznet.net/ ~ kenberry/materials/san-franciscopaper.htm >.

CHAPTER 7: FAMILY ESCAPE STRATEGIES

1. Why didn't you put those shoes in the car?
2. Saxon is a very colorful man. Check him out at < http://www.kurtsaxon.com/ >.
3. I have two different models from Vermont Castings (Encore and Intrepid II), one at each end of the house.
4. Skousen has written several valuable books on designing a secure rural home. Find out more about them at < http://www.joelskousen.com/Secure/securehome.html >.

NOTES

EPILOG: THE FUTURE OF TERROR

1. People naturally ask what else was on the list. The list,
"10 Upcoming Disasters," was accepted by *The People's
Almanac*, and the contract was signed March 25, 1979.
Look what happened. (1) Severe southern California
earthquake. (I'm going to claim the Northridge earthquake of 1994 until a bigger one comes along.) (2)
Mississippi Valley earthquake. (Still waiting.) (3)
Eruption of Mt. St. Helens. (Erupted May 18, 1980.) (4)
Montana forest fire. (Yellowstone fire, 1988.) (5) Polio
epidemic. (Still worried about that one.) (6) Plague epidemic. (Not worried about that one any more.) (7)
Lassa fever epidemic. (Not worried about that one,
either.) (8) Terrorist attack on a U.S. city. (I think
September 11, 2001, qualifies as a hit.) (9) Nuclear
reactor accident. (The March 28, 1979, emergency at
Three Mile Island occurred *three days* after I sold the
list to the People's Almanac.) (10) Nuclear warfare in
some form. (Thankfully no, but a U.S. nuke on
Baghdad would fulfill the prediction.) I count 5 hits
out of 10, and still waiting for polio, the midcontinent
earthquake, and the nuke. My eventual score could be
as high as 8.
2. Lisa Beyer, "Osama's Endgame," *Time* (October 15,
2001), < http://www.time.com/time/magazine/
article/0,9171,1101011015-178412,00.html >.
3. "Divisions evident in Islamic Mideast, N. Africa,"
CNN.com (September 25, 2001), < http://www.
cnn.com/2001/WORLD/meast/09/24/arab.
standpoints/ >.
4. See "Hot Spots," *U.S. News and World Report,* (October
15, 2001, p. 30) for a list of countries where militant
Islam is a political force. Included are Bosnia,
Chechnya, Algeria, Nigeria, Egypt, Sudan, Jordan,
Saudi Arabia, Tajikistan, Uzbekistan, Kyrgyzstan,

Pakistan, India, Bangladesh, Malaysia, Indonesia, and the Philippines. Some would say that World War III has already begun.

5. "President establishes Office of Homeland Security," White House press release (October 8, 2001), < http://www.whitehouse.gov/news/releases/2001/10/20011008.html >.

6. "FBI fails to expose Al Qaida networks," by Daniel McGrory, *London Times* On Line, 3/11/2002 < http://www.the times.co.uk/article/0,,1164-232311,00.html >. Six months after the 9/11 attack, the FBI had arrested more than 1,300 people without finding a single Al Qaida terrorist.

7. Dave Cook, "The Men Behind the Texas Militia Myth at Close Range," *Austin Chronicle,* volume 15, number 9, < http://www.auschron.com/issues/vol15/issue9/pols.militias.html >.

8. For a glance at the mindset, see "Citizen, can I see your ID?" by Al Martin, < http://www.almartinraw.com/column37.html >.

ABOUT THE AUTHOR

Dr. Bruce Clayton received his doctorate in ecology from the University of Montana in 1978 after getting his bachelor's degree in zoology and botany from UCLA in 1972. His scientific specialties were forest fire ecology and biological control.

He is a well-known survival expert, author of *Life After Doomsday, Fallout Survival,* and *Thinking About Survival,* coauthor of *Survival Books* and *Urban Alert,* and formerly the publisher of *The Survivalist Directory.* Dr. Clayton is a fourth-degree black belt instructor in shotokan karate and an expert on improvised weapons.

Dr. Clayton is a state-certified instructor of radiological defense techniques and fallout shelter management in California and has been trained in disaster shelter management and damage assessment by the American Red Cross. He is a former editor of *INFO-RAY,* the newsletter of the

California Radiological Defense Officers' Association and has been a contributing editor to *Survive* magazine, *Survival Guide* magazine, and the *Survival Tomorrow* newsletter. Dr. Clayton was one of the founding members of Doctors for Disaster Preparedness (DDP).

In October 1982, Dr. Clayton was invited to speak at the yearly convention of the U.S. Civil Defense Council (USCDC). Subsequently, the USCDC gave him the Eugene Wigner Award for his work in educating the American public about civil preparedness.

On May 1984, Dr. Clayton received a citation from Governor George Deukmajian of California for "Exceptional Achievement in the field of Emergency Preparedness." The citation reads, in part, "Dr. Clayton has represented the emergency management community with distinction in public forums, where his calm, factual, scientific approach has been highly effective in informing the public about the importance of disaster preparedness."

He has been interviewed by several national television programs, including *The CBS Evening News*, *The Tomorrow Show*, *Today*, and *60 Minutes*, and has appeared on many local radio programs in the United States, Great Britain, Canada, and Australia.

For the record, Dr. Clayton has never been a member of *any* political party, any religious organization, or any group that is based on animosity or intolerance.